World Literature

Excellence in Literature: English 5

Fourth Edition

Janice Campbell

Excellence in Literature: Reading and Writing through the Classics

— Introduction to Literature (English I)

— Literature and Composition (English II)

— American Literature: A Survey Course (English III)

— British Literature: A Survey Course (English IV)

— **World Literature: A Survey Course (English V)**

— The Complete Curriculum (All 5 years in a binder)

— Excellence in Literature *Handbook for Writers*

Fourth Edition: © 2021 Everyday Education, LLC

All rights reserved. No portion of this book may be reproduced or transmitted in any form or by any means without the express written permission of the author or publisher, except for brief quotations in printed reviews. Requests for permission should be made in writing to Everyday Education, LLC.

Everyday Education, LLC
P. O. Box 549
Ashland, VA 23005
www.EverydayEducation.com

Front Cover Art: *School of Athens* by Raphael (Raffaello Sanzio da Urbino), c. 1509–1511

Index of context resource links:

https://excellence-in-literature.com/curriculum-user-content/e5-context-resources/.

Campbell, Janice

British Literature / Excellence in literature: reading and writing through the classics / Janice Campbell

ISBN: 978-1-61322-082-5

1. Literature—Explication. 2. Literature—History and Criticism. 3. Books and reading. I. Title.

It is a great thing to start life with a small number of
really good books
which are your very own.
You may not appreciate them at first.
You may pine for your novel of crude and unadulterated adventure.
You may, and will, give it the preference when you can.
But the dull days come, and the rainy days come,
and always you are driven to fill up the chinks of your reading
with the worthy books which wait so patiently for your notice.
And then suddenly, on a day which marks an epoch in your life,
you understand the difference.
You see, like a flash, how the one stands for nothing,
and the other for literature.
From that day onwards you may return to your crudities,
but at least you do so with some
standard of comparison in your mind.
You can never be the same as you were before.
Then gradually the good thing becomes more dear to you;
it builds itself up with your growing mind;
it becomes a part of your better self, and so,
at last, you can look, as I do now, at the old covers
and love them for all that they have meant in the past.

—Arthur Conan Doyle, *Through the Magic Door*

Thank you!

I would like to offer special thanks to some of my former students,
who graciously agreed to share their work as models.

Erin Bensing

Jonathan Bensing

Lindsey Bensing

Eric Lansing

Rebecca Shealy-Houghton

Jesse Thompson

I would also like to thank the helpers who have contributed time and expertise to
make Excellence in Literature and the accompanying website what they are today.

Taylor Campbell

Rebecca Shealy-Houghton

Craig Campbell

Andrew Bailey

"In ordinary life,
we hardly realize that we receive a great deal more than we give,
and that it is only with gratitude that life becomes rich."

Dietrich Bonhoeffer

Deo gratias.

Contents

Preface 7
Overview and Objectives 9
   How to Benefit from This Guide 10
   Scheduling 11
   Course Format 11
   Prerequisites for Success 13
Getting Started 24
Frequently Asked Questions 29
How to Read a Book 36
   Questions to Consider as You Read 43
How to Write an Essay 44
   The Writing Process 45
   Topic Sentence Outline 48
   Write the Essay 49
Discerning Worldview through Literary Periods 51
Tips for Using EIL in a Classroom 55
Odyssey by Homer (c. 7th–9th century BC) 59
   Context Resources 61
   Assignment Schedule 66
Antigone by Sophocles (496–406 BC) 68
   Context Resources 69
   Assignment Schedule 72
The Aeneid by Virgil (70–19 BC) 75
   Context Resources 77
   Assignment Schedule 81
Inferno by Dante Alighieri (1265–1321) 83
   Context Resources 85
   Assignment Schedule 89
Don Quixote by Miguel de Cervantes (1547–1616) 91
   Context Resources 92
   Assignment Schedule 97

Les Misérables by Victor Hugo (1802–1885) 99
    Context Resources 100
    Assignment Schedule 107

Russian Literature Selections 109
    Context Resources 111
    Assignment Schedule 118

Faust by Johann Wolfgang von Goethe (1749–1832) 120
    Context Resources 121
    Assignment Schedule 128

Out of Africa by Isak Dinesen (1885–1962) 130
    Context Resources 132
    Assignment Schedule 136

Honors 138

Tips for Writing a College-Ready Research Paper 142

Formats and Models 146
    Approach Paper Format 147
    Approach Paper Model 149
    Historical Approach Paper Format 151
    Historical Approach Paper Model 151
    Author Profile Format 153
    Author Profile Model 154
    Literature Summary Format 154
    Literature Summary Model 155
    Literary Analysis Model 155
    Sample Compare/Contrast Essay Model 158
    Sample Poetry Analysis Model 160
    MLA Format Model 162

How to Evaluate Writing 165
    A Constructive Evaluation Starts With a Rubric 165
    Parent Tip: How to Use a Writer's Handbook in Evaluation 166

Excellence in Literature Evaluation Rubric 168

Excellence in Literature: Student Evaluation Summary 169

Glossary 171

Selected Resources 182

Preface

Dear Student,

Do you know that very few people know how to read?

It is not that they cannot decipher words on a page, but they simply do not know how to place what they read into its proper literary and historical context. They may understand WHAT happened in a story, but they do not know WHY. They may feel strongly about the story, yet they never stop to wonder WHY they feel as they do, or HOW the author made it happen.

If you are wondering why you should care about the HOW and WHY of literature, think about it like this: Reading without understanding is like walking onto a softball field and batting the ball, without any knowledge of what to do next. You may hit the ball out of the park, but if you do not run the bases and complete the play, you have missed the whole point of the activity.

It is the same with reading. In order to complete the process, it is necessary to think deeply about what you read. Reading is a conversation between a reader and a writer. The author creates a world, peoples it with characters, and presents a story. The reader enters the author's world, meets the characters, and follows the story line. When you write about literature, as you will this year, the conversation shifts. It becomes a dialogue between you, as an analytical reader and writer, and the reader of your essay.

In this literature curriculum, I'll introduce you to "deep reading," in which you will immerse in a great story, contemplating as you read. In each module, I'll point you toward additional resources such as poetry, art, music, and history. These things will help you understand a bit more about the author, his or her time and place in history, and the cultural influences that shaped the work of literature you are studying.

You will find that you like some books and authors better than others, just as I do. Each novel, poem, essay, or play in this literature series has been carefully chosen for its quality and its place in the panorama of literary history. Even if you find you don't enjoy a particular work as much as another, it has been included because it has something important to convey. One thing you will discover is that sometimes the stories you like least stick with you the longest and sometimes even teach you the most.

I love to read, and I am happy to have the opportunity to share some of my favorite great books with you. Some will make you laugh, others may make you cry, but above all, I hope they make you think. When you finish your reading for the year, I know your mind will be more richly furnished than when you began, and that is a very good thing.

Janice Campbell

www.ExcellenceInLiterature.com

P. S. As you read through this study guide and all the books in EIL, you will most likely encounter words you do not know. I'm sure you know what to do when this happens. Look it up and write down the word and its definition, and you will be expanding your vocabulary without much effort at all!

Overview and Objectives

*In the case of good books, the point is not to see how many of them you can get through,
but rather how many can get through to you.*

–Mortimer J. Alder

Excellence in Literature (EIL) is a college-preparatory course of study. It is my goal to

- Introduce you to great literature from the Western literary tradition.
- Teach you to read with discernment.
- Help you become an independent, self-motivated learner.
- Provide tools you can use to strengthen your writing skills.
- Introduce you to sources for high-quality online and off-line research.
- Prepare you for college classes by expecting you to turn in carefully researched, well-considered writing assignments in the assigned format, with preliminary proofreading completed.

In the five levels of this literature series, you will be reading some of the greatest works of literature ever written. They are great not just because they are technically well done, though that certainly is a factor, but also because they reveal truth through the power of story.

EIL uses great literature, studied in its historic, literary, and artistic contexts, to help you learn to think and write analytically. This book is designed for you, the student, to use independently, so it contains specific instructions for each assignment, and a suggested schedule, as well as the references you need in order to do the background reading and research for each module.

You may be surprised to find I have not provided a lengthy introduction and a lot of background material for each book and author. This is because you have reached the age when you can assume responsibility for learning. Rather than spoon-feeding you basic, easily-researched information (and having you zone out in the middle of paragraph two), I have pointed you to resources and links that will enable you to perform the contextual research needed to more deeply understand the focus text. This is similar to the kind of research you will do for college courses, so if you learn how to do it now, you should be quite good at it by the time you graduate.

How to Benefit from This Guide

There are three main sections in this study guide. Begin by reading the front and back sections first, as they will explain how to use the curriculum. Here's what you will find in each section.

Section I: How to Use the Curriculum

In the first section, you will find an explanation of how EIL works, suggestions for how to create a study routine and organize your study materials, chapters on how to read analytically and how to write essays.

Section II: Modules

Following this you will find the syllabus section, with a study outline and schedule for each module.

Section III: How to Format and Grade Papers

In the final section you will find instructions for writing specific types of papers, information for your writing mentor on how to evaluate papers, and sample papers that demonstrate correct MLA format (if you do not know what that is, be patient—it is explained in the samples and the glossary). Be sure to read all the chapters so you can be successful as you work through the assignments.

Scheduling

Each level of EIL has nine modules. Each module is intended to be completed in four relatively brief, but intense, weeks. Your writing mentor can adapt that schedule for you if needed.

You may choose to group the modules into a traditional nine-month school year, or to use a four weeks on, one week off schedule. For a weekly routine, our family loosely followed a college-style block schedule in which we studied the humanities (literature, history, art, and music) in 2- to 3 hour blocks of time on Tuesday and Thursday; and math, science, and related subjects on Monday and Wednesday, but you are free to do what works best for you and your family.

Each assignment has been carefully chosen and scheduled so that knowledge and skills can build cumulatively, even if your writing mentor changes the order in which you study the modules. It is important that you learn time management skills that will help you complete assignments with minimal stress. If you are working with a writing mentor such as your parent, a writing evaluator, a coach, or a co-op instructor, be sure to agree in advance on a schedule, so that you can plan your work efficiently. Above all, do not spend three weeks procrastinating; then try to cram the assigned reading and writing into one week. Believe me, it does not work!

Course Format

Excellence in Literature courses focus in depth on selected great authors or literary movements, while exploring the context of the author's life and working through additional reading and writing. You'll be able to practice writing in a number of different formats, and to grow thoroughly familiar with some of the greatest writers and literary works of all time.

Audio Books

Although many students are visual learners and do well reading each novel, auditory or kinesthetic learners may benefit from listening to unabridged audio versions of some of the focus texts. Any of the epic poems such as *Beowulf* or *Odyssey* work especially well in audio, as that is how they were enjoyed by the original audiences. It can also be easier to appreciate the rhythm and cadence of the language when you are listening to a good reader. The goal is for you to thoroughly understand and enjoy the material we cover, so use the learning tools that work best for you.

Context Materials

For each module there will be "context resources" — history, art, poetry, and more — to read, listen to, or watch. These will help you understand the focus work. You'll find links to interesting and informative websites, and recommendations for additional readings. Many of these are hosted or linked at Excellence-in-Literature.com; you can view them at the "Study Guide Links" pages on the site.

Do not feel limited by these resource suggestions. I encourage you to find and include other resources, such as videos, field trips, or other useful books. The more rich and varied the context materials, the more you'll learn about the focus text. If you find a book or author you particularly enjoy, take the time to read more of his or her writings and others like them. EIL is a solid foundation, and it is designed to be flexible, so you can shape it to reflect your own interests.

Study Clusters

You may want to consider planning the high school years in study clusters—grouping American history with American literature, British history with British literature, and so forth. This reinforces learning and increases memorable context for both literature and history. You may mix and match EIL modules to fit the history you are studying, though it is wise to remember that the modules graduate in difficulty through the five levels of the curriculum.

The Honors Track

In each module, you will find additional reading suggestions under the "Honors" heading. If you would like to earn an honors-level grade (weighted by .5 grade point), you need to read an extra book and usually do summary titles and an approach paper for each module. At the end of the school year, you will also write an additional research paper, which is assigned in the Honors chapter. This will complete the honors track.

To earn advanced placement or college credit for the class (weighted by 1.0 grade point), you will also need to take an AP or CLEP exam. You can find complete details on how to assign weighted grades and record advanced classes in my book, *Transcripts Made Easy* (www.TranscriptsMadeEasy.com). Additional information about how and why to earn college credits can be found in *Get a Jump Start on College!* (www.GetAJumpStartOnCollege.com).

Prerequisites for Success

Excellence in Literature is intended for use by students in grades 8–12. For each level, you are expected to have age-appropriate skills in grammar, spelling, and language mechanics. You should grammar- and spell-check all papers and refer to a writer's handbook to check your grammar, style, and punctuation before turning in your papers. Learning to self-edit is part of the writing process, and it helps to learn it before you arrive at college or the world of work.

If you have not done much literary analysis or essay writing before EIL, there are a couple of resources you might find helpful. *Teaching the Classics* by Adam and Missy Andrews is a brief DVD course that teaches literary analysis using short works to illustrate the principles and methods. For essay writing, you can use the EIL *Handbook for Writers* recommended to accompany these study guides. If you need an additional resource, *The Elegant Essay Writing Lessons* by Lesha Myers is a solid guide. Either resource can be used concurrently with *Excellence in Literature*.

Learning Philosophy

Learn (lûrn) v. 1 Acquire knowledge of (a subject) or skill in (an art, etc.) as a result of study, experience, or instruction; acquire or develop an ability to do. 4.1 Commit to memory.
—Oxford Shorter English Dictionary

Part of the foundation of the *Excellence in Literature* philosophy is the verb "learn." Learning is an active endeavor, and the main action takes place in one person—the learner. That's you! In this course you'll receive not only knowledge, but you'll also learn to become an active learner. You'll take away study methods and communication skills you can use for many subjects. There is great joy in learning, and this, above all, is what I want to communicate.

The Learning Process: Roles of Excellence in Literature, the Student, and the Writing Mentor

The EIL guide will

- Establish the scope and sequence for the class.
- Assign appropriate readings.
- Provide a suggested schedule for assignments.
- Provide time management and organization tips.
- Provide a rubric for objectively evaluating completed assignments.

The Student will

- Study this book and understand the sequence and timing of assignments.
- Ask questions of the writing mentor when something is not clearly understood.
- Actively seek to learn from each assignment.
- Complete all assignments on time.
- Make no excuses.
- Enjoy great literature.

The Writing Mentor (teacher or parent) will

- Help the student obtain required books and reference materials.
- Verify that assignments are completed on schedule.
- Use the rubric or select a qualified writing evaluator to provide feedback for the student.
- Provide an evaluation summary for the year, using the form found at the end of this book.

Module 5.1 Suggested Schedule

Odyssey

Concepts and Ideas	Writing Types	Poetry
• Conventions of epic poetry • Concepts of honor and cunning • Parallel story lines of Odysseus, Penelope, and Athena	• Event summaries • Historic Approach Paper • Essay OR retelling	• "Reading Poetry" section in the "How to Read a Book" chapter. • C. P. Cavafy • Joseph Brodsky • John Keats

Week	What to Read	What to Write	Honors Reading (optional)	Honors Writing (optional)
1	❏ Module 5.1 in Study Guide ❏ Begin reading *Odyssey* ❏ Context Resources	❏ Event summary for each of the 24 "books" of the *Odyssey*		
2	❏ Continue reading *Odyssey*; finish if possible. ❏ Continue Context resources	❏ Historic Approach Paper		

3	❏ Finish Context resources	❏ Write first draft of a 750-word essay or retelling.
		  ❏ Use the rubric to check your paper
		  ❏ Proofread out loud
		  ❏ Turn it in for evaluation
			❏ *Iliad*	❏ Book summaries
				❏ Approach paper

4	Additional reading ❏ Literary Analysis Essay Instructions (F&M chapter)	❏ Revise your draft based on the rubric and evaluation comments. ❏ Finish, proofread, and turn in your paper.		

Notes:
- You will find complete assignment instructions in the Assignment Schedule for this module.
- The suggested schedule may be adapted to fit your needs; just check off each assignment as you complete it.

Module 5.2 Suggested Schedule				
Antigone				
Concepts and Ideas • Greek Tragedy and the function of the Chorus • The hero's journey • Conflict between duty and authority		**Writing Types** • Author profile • Approach Paper • Essay OR Retelling		**Poetry** • Sophocles • Seamus Heaney • William Butler Yeats
Week	What to Read	What to Write	Honors Reading (optional)	Honors Writing (optional)
1	❏ Module 5.2 in Study Guide ❏ Start reading *Antigone* ❏ Start Context Resources	❏ Author Profile	❏ *Oedipus Rex*	For your chosen works, write ❏ Summary titles ❏ Approach paper
2	❏ Finish reading *Antigone* ❏ Continue Context Resources	❏ Approach Paper		

3	❏ Finish reading, watching, and listening to context resources.	❏ Write first draft of a 750-word essay or retelling
		   ❏ Use the rubric to check your essay or story
		   ❏ Proofread out loud
		   ❏ Turn it in for evaluation		

4	Additional reading ❏ The Burial at Thebes	❏ Revise your draft based on the rubric and evaluation comments. ❏ Finish, proofread, and turn in your paper.		

Notes:
- You will find complete assignment instructions in the Assignment Schedule for this module.
- The Additional Reading recommendations can be found at Excellence-in-Literature.com; use the site search box to go to it.
- The suggested schedule may be adapted to fit your needs; just check off each assignment as you complete it.

Module 5.3 Suggested Schedule

The Aeneid

Concepts and Ideas	Writing Types	Poetry
• Differences between Ancient Greek and Roman societies • Fiction as history • Political ideas that influenced America's Founding Fathers	• Author profile • Summaries OR Storyboard • Essay OR Retelling	• Horace • Martial • Catullus

Week	What to Read	What to Write	Honors Reading (optional)	Honors Writing (optional)
1	❑ Module 5.3 in Study Guide ❑ Start reading *The Aeneid* ❑ Start Context Resources	❑ Author Profile	❑ *Lives of the Noble Grecians and Romans*	❑ Summary titles ❑ Approach paper
2 3	❑ Continue reading *The Aeneid*; finish if possible. ❑ Continue Context resources	❑ Summaries OR ❑ Storyboard		

	❑ Finish reading, watching, and listening to context resources.	❑ Write first draft of a 750-word essay or retelling
		❑ Use the rubric to check your essay
		   ❑ Proofread out loud
		   ❑ Turn it in for evaluation		

4	Additional reading ❑	❑ Revise your draft based on the rubric and evaluation comments. ❑ Finish, proofread, and turn in your paper.		

Notes:
- You will find complete assignment instructions in the Assignment Schedule for this module.
- The suggested schedule may be adapted to fit your needs; just check off each assignment as you complete it.

Module 5.4 Suggested Schedule

The Inferno

Concepts and Ideas	Writing Types	Poetry
• Medieval worldview • Literary use of light and dark • Use of history, biography, and theological concepts in a fictional epic • Literary comedy	• Author profile • Canto Summaries • Essay OR Retelling	• Brunetto Latini • Walther von der Vogelweide • Dante Alighieri

Week	What to Read	What to Write	Honors Reading (optional)	Honors Writing (optional)
1	❏ Module 5.4 in Study Guide ❏ Start reading or listening to *Inferno* ❏ Start Context Resources	❏ Author Profile	❏ *Purgatorio* AND/OR *Paradiso* OR ❏ *Confessions* by Augustine	❏ Summary titles ❏ Approach paper
2	❏ Continue *Inferno*; finish if possible ❏ Continue Context resources	❏ Canto Summaries		

3	❏ Finish all reading, watching, and listening to context resources.	❏ Write a first draft of a 750-word paper
		  ❏ Use the rubric to check your paper
		  ❏ Proofread out loud
		  ❏ Turn it in for evaluation		

4	❏ Additional reading	❏ Revise your draft based on the rubric and evaluation comments. ❏ Finish, proofread, and turn in your paper.		

Notes:
- You will find complete assignment instructions in the Assignment Schedule for this module.
- The suggested schedule may be adapted to fit your needs; just check off each assignment as you complete it.

Module 5.5 Suggested Schedule

Don Quixote

Concepts and Ideas	**Writing Types**	**Poetry**
• Picaresque novel tradition • The significance of reading • Spanish Golden Age	• Author profile • Book summaries • Essay or Journalistic Articles	• G. K. Chesterton • Francisco de Quevedo • Luis de Góngora

Week	What to Read	What to Write	Honors Reading (optional)	Honors Writing (optional)
1	❏ Module 5.5 in Study Guide ❏ Start *Don Quixote* ❏ Start Context Resources	❏ Author profile	❏ *The Pickwick Papers* by Dickens	❏ Summary titles ❏ Approach paper
2	❏ Continue reading *Don Quixote;* finish if possible ❏ Continue Context resources	❏ Book summaries		

3	❏ Finish reading, watching, and listening to context resources.	❏ Write first draft of a 750-word paper
		  ❏ Use the rubric to check your essay
		  ❏ Proofread out loud
		  ❏ Turn it in for evaluation		

4	Additional reading ❏	❏ Revise your draft based on the rubric and evaluation comments. ❏ Finish, proofread, and turn in your paper.		

Notes:
• You will find complete assignment instructions in the Assignment Schedule for this module.
• The suggested schedule may be adapted to fit your needs; just check off each assignment as you complete it.

Module 5.6 Suggested Schedule

Les Misérables

Concepts and Ideas	Writing Types	Poetry
• Transition from Romantic to Realist literature • The nature and power of justice, mercy, and love • Injustice as a cause of revolution or rebellion	• Author profile • Approach paper • Essay or series of letters	• Victor Hugo • Alphonse de Lamartine • Marceline Desbordes-Valmore

Week	What to Read	What to Write	Honors Reading (optional)	Honors Writing (optional)
1	❏ Module 5.6 in Study Guide ❏ Start reading *Les Misérables* ❏ Start Context Resources	❏ Author Profile	❏ *The Hunchback of Notre Dame* OR *Democracy in America*	❏ Summary titles ❏ Approach paper
2	❏ Continue *Les Misérables*; finish if possible ❏ Continue Context resources	❏ Approach Paper		

3	❏ Finish reading, watching, and listening to context resources.	❏ Write first draft of a 750-word essay or series of letters
		  ❏ Use the rubric to check your essay
		  ❏ Proofread out loud
		  ❏ Turn it in for evaluation		

4	Additional reading	❏ Revise your draft based on the rubric and evaluation comments. ❏ Finish, proofread, and turn in your paper.		

Notes:
- You will find complete assignment instructions in the Assignment Schedule for this module.
- The suggested schedule may be adapted to fit your needs; just check off each assignment as you complete it.

Module 5.7 Suggested Schedule

Russian Literature Selections

Concepts and Ideas	Writing Types	Poetry
• Transition from Romanticism to Realism • Effect of historical events on literary style and themes • Strong connections between art, music, and literary themes • Comparison of Russian, British, and American experiences/themes	• Author profiles • Historical Approach Paper • Essay	• Aleksandr Pushkin • Anna Akhmatova

Week	What to Read	What to Write	Honors Reading (optional)	Honors Writing (optional)
1	❏ Module 5.7 in Study Guide ❏ Begin reading the Russian selections ❏ Start Context Resources	❏ Author Profiles		
2	❏ Finish reading the assigned works ❏ Continue Context resources	❏ Historical Approach Paper	❏ *The Brothers Karamazov* OR *Crime and Punishment* OR *The Gulag Archipelago*	❏ Summary titles ❏ Approach paper

3	❏ Finish reading, watching, and listening to context resources.	❏ Write first draft of a 750-word paper
		  ❏ Use the rubric to check your paper
		  ❏ Proofread out loud
		  ❏ Turn it in for evaluation		

4	Additional reading	❏ Revise your draft based on the rubric and evaluation comments. ❏ Finish, proofread, and turn in your paper.		

Notes:
- You will find complete assignment instructions in the Assignment Schedule for this module.
- The suggested schedule may be adapted to fit your needs; just check off each assignment as you complete it.

Module 5.8 Suggested Schedule

Faust

Concepts and Ideas	Writing Types	Poetry
• The influence of Romanticism • Sturm und Drang • The idea of a Faustian bargain • Adaptation of older fable, myth, or legend into a new work • Themes of light and darkness	• Author profile • Approach paper or letter • Literary analysis essay	• Johann von Goethe • Friedrich Schiller • George Gordon, Lord Byron

Week	What to Read	What to Write	Honors Reading (optional)	Honors Writing (optional)
1	❏ Module 5.8 in Study Guide ❏ Start reading *Faust* ❏ Start Context Resources	❏ Author Profile		
2	❏ Continue reading *Faust* ❏ Continue Context resources	❏ Approach paper or letter	❏ *The Screwtape Letters* AND *The Picture of Dorian Grey* OR ❏ *Frankenstein* OR ❏ *Doctor Faustus*	❏ Scene Summaries ❏ Approach paper
3	❏ Finish reading, watching, and listening to context resources.	❏ Write first draft of a 750-word essay 　❏ Use the rubric to check your paper 　❏ Proofread out loud 　❏ Turn it in for evaluation		
4	Additional reading	❏ Revise your draft based on the rubric and evaluation comments. ❏ Finish, proofread, and turn in your paper.		

Notes:
• You will find complete assignment instructions in the Assignment Schedule for this module.
• The suggested schedule may be adapted to fit your needs; just check off each assignment as you complete it.

Module 5.9 Suggested Schedule

Out of Africa

Concepts and Ideas	Writing Types	Poetry
• Storytelling vs. memoir or autobiography • Literature as a cultural bridge • Colonialism and its effects	• Author profile • Creative Retelling • Essay	• A. E. Housman • Rainer Maria Rilke • Marianne Moore

Week	What to Read	What to Write	Honors Reading (optional)	Honors Writing (optional)
1	❏ Module 5.9 in Study Guide ❏ Start reading *Out of Africa* ❏ Start Context Resources	❏ Author Profile		
2	❏ Finish *Out of Africa* ❏ Continue Context resources	❏ Creative Retelling	❏ *Cry the Beloved Country* OR *Surprised by Joy*	❏ Summary titles ❏ Approach paper

3	❏ Finish reading, watching, and listening to context resources.	❏ Write first draft of a 750-word essay
		  ❏ Use the rubric to check your paper
		  ❏ Proofread out loud
		  ❏ Turn it in for evaluation		

4	Additional reading ❏ *Babette's Feast*	❏ Revise your draft based on the rubric and evaluation comments. ❏ Finish, proofread, and turn in your paper.		

Notes:
- You will find complete assignment instructions in the Assignment Schedule for this module.
- The suggested schedule may be adapted to fit your needs; just check off each assignment as you complete it.

Getting Started

"The main thing I try to do is write as clearly as I can. I rewrite a good deal to make it clear."
— E. B. White

Before you begin, set up a study area and English notebook to help you stay organized. If you learn how to do this now, you will be a step ahead when you get to college and realize that you are completely responsible for creating a time and place to learn. College professors usually hand out a syllabus at the first class, with all the assignments and due dates for the semester. They do not remind you of what is coming up, so if you do not have a method for keeping on top of everything, you can quickly fall behind. You will find the organizational techniques you learn from EIL helpful for any class you take in the future.

What belongs in a study area?

Study area basics are a comfortable chair, bright light, your English notebook and reading log, calendar or datebook, good dictionary, thesaurus, the EIL *Handbook for Writers* or other writer's handbook, pens, pencils, paper, sticky notes such as Post-it® notes, and possibly a computer. Being organized will make your study time more pleasant and productive, so be sure to start the school year by pulling together these things.

How to Use Items in Your Study Area

Chair and light: Read here (see the chapter on "How to Read a Book"). You want to be comfortable enough to enjoy the experience, but not so comfortable that you fall asleep. It is pleasant to read near a window, but you should also have a reading light positioned so that the light falls on your book. If you find that your eyes get tired quickly, you may need a brighter light or even reading glasses. Do not hesitate to get your eyes checked, so you can enjoy reading.

Calendar: Use a calendar or planner to record assignment deadlines, field trips, and other activities. At the beginning of each module, check the number of pages in your focus text and number of context resources; then plan how many you need to read daily in order to finish the focus text before you begin the essay.

English and Vocabulary notebook: Organize your English papers and vocabulary notes in a three-ring binder. The first page of your notebook should be an index page of the contents. You may make this as you add things, or use a copy of the Student Evaluation Summary in the back of this study guide as index starter. Next, put in a copy of each assignment you do, along with any mind-map or other note pages you'd like to keep and the evaluation rubrics you receive. Make a vocabulary section at the end of the binder (or tuck a small notebook into the pocket on the inside of the cover) with any new words and definitions you learn from each book. You may write these down in the order you discover them, or you may alphabetize them. The main thing is to remember them.

Commonplace book: Use a small blank notebook for copying beautiful or interesting passages from the books you read. I like notebooks with a dot grid as they help me keep my lines straight, but are less obtrusive than lines if I want to add a bit of calligraphy or copy a small sketch from the book. Choose what works for you. I keep a small Moleskine or Field Notes notebook in my purse and a larger (A5 or 5 x 8") Rhodia notebook in my planner so I can write down or read favorite quotes at any time.

Reading log: List everything you read—not just the books you read for English, but everything. Write the title, author, a one- or two-sentence summary of the book, and a comment and a rating. You may use the small *Reading Log* booklets I have on my web-store, EverydayEducation.com, or if you prefer to write lengthy reviews, you may prefer a blank journal.

Dictionary: Look up unfamiliar words you encounter. If you can guess their meaning from the context, just write down the word on a small sticky note and stick it on the page. Look it up after you are finished reading. If you cannot guess the meaning from the context, look it up before continuing. Looking up challenging words not only builds vocabulary and helps you remember the word, but also reveals the nuances in meaning that set the word apart from its synonyms. My favorite dictionary is the *Oxford Shorter English Dictionary* because most of the word usage examples are from literature. Many college dictionaries are acceptable as well.

Thesaurus: Use this when you find yourself repeating the same descriptive words over and over. I use *Roget A to Z*, which is organized alphabetically. The English language is fascinating, and there is a perfect word for almost any occasion—please find it and use it!

EIL *Handbook for Writers* or other handbook: Can't remember when to use a comma or a semicolon? Here is where you go to find out. Need instructions for how to write an expository essay? You will find it in your writer's handbook. A professional writer or editor always has several frequently used handbooks nearby. Writer's handbooks are packed with great information, and the reason professionals have several is that different handbooks have different areas of focus. No matter how competent you are as a writer, it is unlikely that you can remember every tiny detail of grammar, style, or usage, so it pays to check your handbook—chances are, you will find exactly the help you need.

Pens: Use a pen for mind mapping (thinking on paper) rough drafts, illustrations, Venn diagrams, and more. When I was in college, one of my favorite ways to study a long, challenging work was to use an 18" x 24" sketch pad and multi colored gel pens. I spent one semester in an in-depth independent study of Edmund Spenser's *The Fairie Queene* and found that the best way to see themes and remember what happened where was to summarize each book of the poem with a quick sketch (stick figures) and bullet points illustrating each canto.

Pencils: These are for writing in your books. Yes, I mean it—I want you to underline key passages, talk back to the characters, note thoughts that occur to you as you read, and so forth. This is called annotation, and it is part of active reading (you will learn more about this in the "How to Read a Book" chapter). Taking notes in the text will help you get the most out of a story. If you have to use library books for your focus texts, you will not be able to annotate as easily, but you can put a piece of paper in the back of the book and use it for the things you would normally write in the book.

Sticky notes: One of the first things to do is to make sticky-note tabs for your writer's handbook. This helps you turn quickly to key pages. For classes using an anthology, I recommend that at the beginning of the semester you look at the syllabus and go through the anthology and place a sticky-note tab with the author's last name and the title of the work beside each assigned piece. This saves time and helps remind you of what you have covered, and what remains.

Computer: When you reach college or the business world, you will need to know how to use a computer, so high school is the time to become comfortable with its basic functions. Rather than using a word-processing program on your computer, I suggest learning to use the free online word-processing program by Google. It is accessible through any Internet-connected computer, and your paper can be easily shared with a writing instructor, no matter where he or she is located.

Computer Tips

Formatting papers: Once you are in high school, all written work should be submitted in a college-style format. This means it should be typed in Times New Roman or a similar font, double-spaced, with one-inch margins all around (see the sample MLA paper in the back of this book). Be sure to have the grammar- and spell-check turned on in your word-processing program, but don't rely too heavily on these checking tools, because they are often wrong. Always do a "human proofread" by reading your paper aloud to yourself before turning it in. Reading aloud helps you slow down enough to spot typos and hear sentences or phrases that do not flow smoothly.

One space after terminal punctuation: Space only once after any terminal punctuation (period, question mark, etc.). Old typing instruction books used to require two spaces after terminal punctuation because typewriters use what is called a mono-spaced type, and the double spacing helped the eye distinguish the end of a sentence. Computer fonts are proportionally spaced, and proper spacing is programmed in. Double spacing creates unattractive blobs of white down a page and is a dead giveaway that outdated methods are being used.

Saving your document: Always create a computer folder for each class, and use a descriptive file name when you save your papers. For example, if you are writing the essay on Benjamin Franklin's *Autobiography* from the first module of *American Literature*, name the file "eil3-m1-franklin," and it will be easy to find anytime you need it.

If a paper gets "lost" on your computer: If you are new to the world of computers, you may occasionally think you have lost something on your computer. If you have been typing and your text seems to disappear, try pressing the Command key along with Z. This is the "undo" command, and it will undo the last thing you did, which should bring your paper back into view. If it does not, you can search your hard drive for the file name you used when you saved it. If you are using a Mac computer or Google Docs, any document should easily be found.

Frequently Asked Questions

Be curious always! For knowledge will not acquire you; you must acquire it.
—Sudie Back

If you have questions about any aspect of the curriculum or about studying in general, you may find the answers in this chapter.

Are all assignment instructions contained in this book?

This EIL guide contains the outline of the course, an assignment schedule for each module, models of the type of papers you will be writing, and evaluation information. In addition, you will need a copy of each of the novel-length focus works and a writer's handbook.

It is helpful to have old editions of Norton Anthologies of American, British, and World Literature for additional information and readings for each historical period. Beyond the basics, an atlas, art history book, and a dictionary of allusions are excellent optional additions to the study and reference tools listed here and in the "Getting Started" chapter.

You do not tell me how many pages to read each day. How will I know?

It is all about time management! This is a college-prep class, so you will be learning to look ahead and pace yourself. For modules based upon a novel-length work, you have a couple of options: 1) Sit down the first day and read the whole book in several hours; then use the rest of the time to gather supporting information; perhaps read another book by the author; and write your essay; or 2) Divide the book into two equal parts, and read one part per week, leaving the last two weeks to write and polish your essay. I prefer the first method, as the story is usually more interesting if it is not read in tiny fragments over a long period of time. This also leaves plenty of time to draft, revise, and polish your essay.

C. S. Lewis wrote that "a narrative style is not to be judged by snippets. You must read for at least half a day and read with your mind on the story" (from *English Literature in the Sixteenth Century Excluding Drama*). He is a wise guide, because immersion changes the experience of reading from an assignment to a journey into another world, another place, and another time. Whatever you do, start reading the first day of the module, and read every day until the book is finished. Do not procrastinate. And do not forget your context readings!

Can I use library books, or do I have to buy them?

I encourage active reading that includes annotation, especially of the focus works. This means underlining and making notes in the margin, and librarians really hate that. So I recommend you buy the focus books. You can probably find used copies fairly cheaply.

Is it better to own or to borrow books?

I have discovered that if you have books in your home, they will be read. I do not expect you to purchase all the resources I have referenced, but I hope you will consider having a few of the most important on hand. You can find them used at online retailers such as Amazon.com or Alibris.com, or you may even be able to get them free through PaperbackSwap.com (you may use my referral, "readbx"). I have purchased many books quite cheaply from library sales, thrift shops, and yard sales. Studies have shown that the number of books owned in a family has a direct relationship to the student's long-term academic success, with measurably higher test scores for book owners than for age mates with fewer books in the home.

Do you recommend a particular edition of each book?

It is important to have books that are pleasant to hold and read so that you enjoy the process and do not suffer from eyestrain. I do not recommend mass-market paperbacks, since they usually have too-small type, very small margins, and no scholarly introduction or discussion questions. Many are so hard to hold open that the spine is soon broken.

My favorite editions include Ignatius Critical Editions (best notes), Modern Library Paperback Classics. Norton, Penguin, and Oxford. The newest editions from these publishers are designed to lie open like a hardback, and they usually have insightful introductions and good discussion questions at the end. You will find links to each of my recommended editions at ExcellenceinLiterature.com.

Can I read the focus texts on an e-reader?

You can read the texts on an e-reader such as the Kindle® or Nook®, but it is not always easy to annotate as you are reading or to page back to look up a character or event. In addition, if you use free versions from the public domain, be aware that the available translations may not be of the best quality. If you decide to use an e-reader, be sure to learn how to highlight and add notes and bookmarks.

The assignment said to write a 500-word essay. I accidentally wrote 603 words. What shall I do?

You can edit to make your work tighter, which will usually make your paper better. As Strunk and White admonish in *Elements of Style*, it is best to "omit needless words." The second option is to not worry about it. The word count is a minimum rather than a maximum requirement. It is stated as number of words rather than number of pages so that teachers will not receive essays with 16-point type and 2" margins, because someone had to fill three pages and had no ideas. Word count allows no fudging.

What should go into the assignment header?

Every paper you turn in should have a proper heading as shown in the sample papers in the Formats and Models chapter. The heading should include your first and last name, the class name with the instructor's name on the same line, the date, and the essay prompt. The essay prompt is included to make it easy for the evaluator to determine whether your essay is on topic, and it is especially important for modules in which you have a choice of topics.

How do I download and print items from the Internet?

If you have done some Internet research, or if I have provided a link or URL to a resource you want to download and print, you can follow these steps:

1. If you have an ebook of EIL, you should be able to copy the URL from the text. Just copy (control + c) the entire URL, and paste (control + v) it into the address window of your browser, and click "enter."
2. If the page that appears offers a link to a printable copy, click the link to print directly from the screen.
3. If there is no link to a printable copy, hold down the left button of your mouse, and drag to select the text you want to copy.
4. Copy and paste the text into a blank TextEdit or Notepad file, and save it to your English folder or to a Google Drive or Evernote.com account online.
5. Go back to the web page where you found the information. Select the URL in the address line, and copy and paste it at the end of your text. Type in the date you accessed the website and any other information you think may be important. You may need some of this information for your Works Cited page.
6. Remember that it is never okay to copy material from anywhere and turn it in as your own work—this is called plagiarism, and it is a form of stealing. These suggestions are simply intended to help you if you need to save study resources you plan to quote in your essays or research paper.

Why are there a lot of Internet resources?

First, they are free and globally available. If you do not have a computer with Internet access, chances are that you can use one at your local library or at a friend's house. Second, you need to know how to use a computer responsibly, and how to find the kind of resources you will need for the future, whether that future involves college, business, or teaching your own children.

As you use EIL, you will encounter many useful sites and resources. You'll begin to see what is available online, and be able to recognize reliable sites for research. For several years, we have been adding good resources to our own Excellence-in-Literature.com website, so that's a great place to start your literary research.

What happens if a link does not work?

The context resource links are kept updated on the "Study Guide Links" pages at Excellence-in-Literature.com. If a link does not work for you, just type a few words of the title or author's name in the site search box at Excellence-in-Literature.com, and the resource should show up.

If you are typing in links and an EIL resource does not load, double-check each character you have typed and make sure it exactly matches the link provided. If you are using an e-book and you copy and paste the link, be sure not to pick up any punctuation near the link because that will keep it from working. If an online resource has been removed from its original site, we will have provided an appropriate alternative on the "Study Guide Links" pages.

Remember, if you don't find what you are looking for at the provided link, you can always do a search using keywords mentioned in the resource. For example, if you want to see more of the Mark Twain House and Museum, type "mark twain house museum" into your browser's search box, and you will find more resources and photos on that topic.

Do I have to read everything?

There are two things you absolutely must read, and they are this entire guide and each of the focus texts. I would like for you to read most of the context materials, but in a few cases there are more than you need. I have often included more than one suggested biography, simply because there are several good ones to choose from, and you may pick whichever one is easily available. The goal is for you to learn what you need to know in order to understand the author and the text and to write a thoughtful essay, not to just check off a random bunch of stuff.

I thought this was English class. Why do I have to look at art and listen to music?

Literature is a unique representation of its culture. Each great work was written by an author who was influenced by books, people, art, music, and events of his or her day. These influences, coupled with the author's education and family life, shaped the worldview that is inevitably reflected in their work.

In order to understand a poem, play, or story, it helps to understand a bit about the author and his or her philosophy of life. The biographical sketches can help with this, but sampling the art and music the author could have seen or heard is a different and sometimes more compelling way of gaining insight. The sights and sounds of an era can also help to illuminate the philosophy of life that shaped the focus text. You can think of content exploration as a virtual field trip!

How much time will EIL take each day?

The amount of time you spend depends on the length of the focus text and your reading speed. As an average, plan to spend at least one hour per day reading or writing about the focus text. Separate context reading or vocabulary work may add an additional 20–45 minutes per day.

Our family is different—do we have to follow the schedule exactly as it is written?

The schedule I have provided is the one my students followed when I taught these courses online (which I no longer do). It works efficiently and will help you enjoy all the books over the course of the school year. In addition, I arranged the modules to provide variation in type of reading and writing, and the modules graduate in difficulty from the beginning to the end of the year. However, I completely understand that each situation is unique. You may change the schedule, drop a module, take two years to cover the book, or alter it in any way that will help it better serve your family.

If you are teaching EIL in a co-op or school, you have the same liberty, though students who are following along in the book can probably be counted on to remind you that "That's not what Mrs. Campbell said to do!" Whatever you do, I promise that the EIL Enforcement Department will *not* stop by to rap your knuckles. The curriculum is here to serve you, and I want you to enjoy using it.

Why read old books?

There are many reasons to read old books, but author and apologist C. S. Lewis simply suggests that it is necessary in order to "keep the clean sea breeze of the centuries blowing through our minds" and to escape the "characteristic blindness of the twentieth century." He writes:

> It is a good rule, after reading a new book, never to allow yourself another new one till you have read an old one in between. If that is too much for you, you should at least read one old one to every three new ones.
>
> Every age has its own outlook. It is specially good at seeing certain truths and specially liable to make certain mistakes. We all, therefore, need the books that will correct the characteristic mistakes of our own period. And that means the old books. All contemporary writers share to some extent the contemporary outlook—even those, like myself, who seem most opposed to it . . . The only palliative is to keep the clean sea breeze of the centuries blowing through our minds, and this can be done only by reading old books . . . Two heads are better than one, not because either is infallible, but because they are unlikely to go wrong in the same direction.

(C. S. Lewis included these thoughts in his introduction to a translation of *Athanasius: On the Incarnation*. You may read more of the introduction by looking at the "Search Inside" feature for this book at Amazon.com.)

In an article on the Augustine College website, Professor Dominic Manganiello, D.Phil., concurs: "We will read old books, then, because in the past lie the foundations of our present and future hope. We will discover that the writings of the masters deal with 'primal and conventional things . . . the hunger for bread, the love of woman, the love of children, the desire for immortal life.'"

Finally, in perhaps the most compelling reason of all, Alexandr Solzhenitsyn pointed out that "literature conveys irrefutable condensed experience in yet another invaluable direction; namely, from generation to generation. Thus it becomes the living memory of the nation. Thus it preserves and kindles within itself the flame of her spent history, in a form which is safe from deformation and slander. In this way literature, together with language, protects the soul of the nation." You may read his entire 1970 Nobel Lecture at https://www.nobelprize.org/prizes/literature/1970/solzhenitsyn/lecture/.

How to Read a Book

If you don't have time to read, you don't have the time (or the tools) to write. Simple as that.
— Stephen King

No, you have not picked up the wrong course by mistake—this is indeed high school English! I know you have been reading for years, but I want to encourage you to learn to read deeply and thoughtfully. In this brief chapter I will review the way we approach excellent literature and give you tips on how to read well.

Reading is not about skimming over the words on a page. To read well is to enter in to the literature as into a work of art. In *An Experiment in Criticism*, C. S. Lewis suggests that we must "Look. Listen. Receive. Get yourself out of the way." He is right—we study great literature to learn and grow, not to impose contemporary ideas or criticisms upon it. As you read, you will encounter unfamiliar and possibly uncomfortable or unpleasant ideas, characters, or places. Instead of making a snap judgment about these things, consider why they are uncomfortable or unpleasant. What happens because of them, to them, or in them? This is the kind of immersion and contemplation that will help you grow as a reader and writer.

Reading Deeply

The difference between reading well and reading badly is like the difference between settling down to a leisurely and delicious steak dinner or gobbling a dry rice cake on the go. If you want to read well, you will neither rush nor gobble. A reader who reads well will close a finished book with traces of that book engraved in memory.

When you are ready to read, settle down in a quiet, comfortable spot with good light. Read without interruption, and seek to be a true reader, as C. S. Lewis describes it. He explains that "the true reader reads . . . whole-heartedly [and] makes himself as receptive as he can" (*An Experiment in Criticism*). In addition, the true reader must, as Alexander Pope admonished, read "in the same spirit that the author writ." If you are reading something serious, take it seriously; if it's light, take it lightly.

> *Read Receptively*
>
> A work of . . . art can be either "received" or "used." When we "receive" it we exert our senses and imagination and various other powers according to a pattern invented by the artist.
>
> C. S. Lewis

Reading good books can spark a variety of ideas and reflections. We aren't reading classics just to find out what happened, though that is part of it. We are reading them in order to enter into the experiences of another life; to discover what it is like to be entrusted with a quest or to live orphaned and alone. We read them to journey from burning Troy to Carthage and Italy with Aeneas or down the Mississippi River with Huck and Jim.

Books that have stood the test of time do so because they are such evocative portals into these other lives, times, and places. As you read, allow yourself to enter into the story with your imagination and all five senses. Smell the salt air of the wine-dark sea of Odysseus, and hear the creaking of oars and the splashing of waves. Imagine pangs of hunger and weakness so desperate that you are driven to ask a stranger for the porridge meant for a pig (*Jane Eyre*) or to steal a loaf of bread for which you spend years in a terrible prison (*Les Miserables*). To read is to enter in.

Reading Challenging Literature

Some books are meant to be tasted, some swallowed, and some few digested . . .
—Francis Bacon

The classics tell some of the most interesting, thought-provoking stories of all time. The challenge is that if you're haven't read many older books, they can seem difficult, or perhaps even dull because the storytelling style and pacing are difference from what we are accustomed to in the modern era. Readers in earlier centuries expected authors to create vividly detailed stories that allowed the reader to experience the story as if they were there, while many modern readers simply expect to breeze quickly through a book to find out what happened. As you've learned, breezing through is not what leads to reading well.

Here are a few suggestions to help you become more comfortable with older or more challenging books.

- **Immerse**: The key to enjoying any great book is to approach it first as a story. Read or listen all the way through, just as you would if you were reading *The Lord of the Rings* or any other book you enjoy.
- **Don't gobble**: Read all the way through, at a comfortable pace. Read fast enough to sustain interest, but slowly enough to understand what is happening. Seek to be immersed in the story; to see through the eyes of each character.
- **Use training wheels**: For the most challenging books, you may begin by reading a children's version or a brief synopsis of the work. This is not necessary for most works, but I have assigned it for those with archaic language, such as Chaucer's *Canterbury Tales* or for epic poetry such as Homer's *Odyssey*. Once you have read the synopsis or children's version of a difficult book, you will be ready to read or listen to the complete text.
- **Listen or watch**: If the assignment is poetry or a play, listen to it (even if you have to read it aloud to yourself in order to do so) or watch it as suggested in the assignments. Poetry is meant to be heard, and plays are meant to be seen and heard, so you must do this in order to fully appreciate them.
- **Gain insight**: Use the context resources to get acquainted with the history, art, music, poetry, and other literature relevant to the author or focus text. This helps you understand the author's artistic and cultural influences and can give you insight as to why the author wrote the story he/she wrote in the way that it is written.
- **Vocabulary**: As you read, keep an index card or piece of paper tucked into the back of the book, or write on the blank end pages. When you encounter words you do not know, do not interrupt the flow of the story as long as you understand the basic meaning from the context—just write down the word, look it up later, and add it to the list in your English notebook.
- **Annotate**: In your English notebook write down interesting insights that occur to you, as well as quotes that seem significant. Feel free to mark

important or interesting passages in the book (see the "Annotating" section later in this chapter) so that you can easily find them again while writing your essay.

- **Short writing assignments**: Once you have read the book, start the writing assignments. If you are working with a book not listed in this guide, write an approach paper according to the instructions in the Formats and Models chapter. The approach paper should include a brief summary, character analysis, discussion questions, key passage, and an explanation of the key passage. This will help you think through the book and prepare you for writing an essay.

- **Essay**: Write the assigned essay in response to the essay prompt. Believe it or not, writing thoughtfully about something specific in the book helps you gain insights you wouldn't otherwise have. Writing helps you learn!

Freytag's Pyramid: The Shape of a Story

Did you know that the action in a plot can be visualized as a shape? German novelist Gustav Freytag created a diagram to show the form of a basic plot. Here is a simple example of Freytag's Pyramid, followed by brief definitions of each stage.

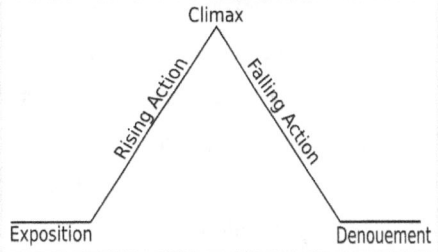

- Exposition: Here's where the scene is set, characters introduced, and the situation established. It usually falls at the beginning of the book, but additional exposition is often scattered throughout the work.

- Rising Action: Things get complicated in this section, with the conflict intensifying or even multiplying (think of a mystery in which more crimes are committed as detectives try to solve the first crime).

- Climax: The turning point in fiction; the transition from rising to falling action.

- Falling Action: Here's where the problems encountered during the rising action are solved.

- Denouement: Resolution or conclusion.

Reading Fiction

If you are reading fiction, you will need to notice how the elements of **plot, theme, character, setting, and style** work together with **point of view** to create the alternate world of the story. However, as discussed in "Reading Deeply," it is also important to allow yourself to be immersed in the fictional world to the point that when you stop reading, you feel as if you have just returned from a long journey. Immersion makes it easier to see the story as a whole so that as you read you will recognize where you are in the plot. If the protagonist (the hero) is in terrible trouble, you're in the midst of conflict. If all the loose ends of the story are being wrapped up, you've made it past the climax and are at the point of falling action, moving toward denouement.

If you are reading through the book with someone else, it can help to consider and discuss a few questions from the list at the end of this chapter. These are designed to help you move deeper into the text and prepare for the writing assignments. If the questions contain literary terms you don't know, look them up in the Glossary of this guide. If you need more information, consult your writer's handbook, check Excellence-in-Literature.com, or go to Google and type in "define:" (without the quotes) followed by the word or phrase you are looking for.

Reading Poetry

There is poetry in almost every module. Reading poetry is a bit different from reading prose (writing that is not poetry). Poetry uses structure, sound, and syntax to awaken the reader's imagination and to convey an image or message in a vivid and memorable way. A beautifully written poem can convey an idea in just a few unforgettable lines.

If you have not studied the analysis of poetry, it is especially important to review the process in one or more of the resources I have recommended. If you have the *Handbook for Writers* from EIL, you'll find a discussion of how to read and write about lyric poetry in Part 1: Section 10.8. Another resource you might find helpful is *Working it Out* by Joseph Womack. This little book offers a year-long study of the poetry of George Herbert, and in the process, demonstrates a simple and effective method for delving more deeply into any poem.

For now, here's how to begin understanding a poem. Start by reading it through slowly and carefully at least once or twice. Read it aloud, and listen to the sound of the words and pacing of the lines and syllables. Once you have the sound of the poem in your head, try paraphrasing it in prose. Think about each element and how the structure of the lines and the sound of the words contributes to the poem's theme. Examine the images, the rhyme scheme, and the sound patterns of the poem to help you understand the poet's message. Above all, read it through (or listen to it) in its entirety often enough that you see and remember it as a whole, just as you would look at a great painting as a whole before beginning to study the brush strokes.

Comedy and Tragedy

Although we sometimes think of comedy as something funny and tragedy as something sad, these words have a slightly different meaning in the study of literature. Comedy is a story that begins with a conflict or suffering and ends in joy, such as *Jane Eyre* or *A Midsummer Night's Dream*.

Tragedy is a story that begins at a high point and ends in pain, such as *Romeo and Juliet* or *Oedipus Rex*. In Veith's interesting chapter on comedy and tragedy, he suggests that the upward movement in comedy reflects a redemptive storyline, while the downward movement of tragedy reflects the archetypal fall of humanity. Aristotle further defined tragedy as the downfall of a noble human, in a disaster of his own making (*King Lear*).

Facing Challenging Ideas

Great literature tends to mirror life. A book becomes a classic because it creates an honest and true picture of life and accurately depicts the consequences of various philosophies of life. In portraying life accurately, complex and sometimes unpleasant issues arise, just as they do in life. Characters do or say things that are deeply wrong, as Macbeth did in giving way to ambition and committing murder, or less seriously, as Peter Rabbit did in stealing carrots from Mr. MacGregor's garden. However, each character experienced appropriate, true-to-life consequences for his actions, rather than an awkwardly contrived happy end. This is how literature can reflect life.

Gene Edward Veith specifically cautions conservative readers not to "seize upon a detail [such as a "bad word"] or a subject dealt with in a book, take it completely out of context, and fail to do the necessary labor of thinking about the work and interpreting it thematically" (72) before taking a stand against the book. He also cautions against stories that do not tell the truth about life. "Stories filled with 'good people' overcoming all odds may create the dangerous impression that human beings are, in fact, 'good' and capable of saving themselves through their own moral actions" (76). This type of plot is often found in genre fiction—what I call "Twinkies® for the brain"—and is what keeps these books from being great literature even when they tell an enjoyable story.

Annotating: Please Write in Your Books!

If you annotate your books as you read, you will understand and enjoy them more deeply than if you simply skim the text. Your annotations will also help you quickly locate important scenes in the book as you are doing the writing assignments for each module. Here are some suggestions for effective annotation.

- **Use a pencil** for writing in your books, as it does not show through and can be erased if necessary.
- Use the inside of the covers or the blank pages at the front and back for notes. Use an index card or piece of paper if you are using a library book.
- **Draw a vertical line** or star beside significant paragraphs.
- **Underline** important phrases or ideas.
- **Character List:** Use the inside of the front cover to list each of the characters in the order in which they appear. Include a brief note about the character's role in the plot or any distinguishing characteristics.
- **Timeline**: List each major event in the story as it happens. The inside back cover is a good place for this.
- **Sketch** small illustrations or write in subheadings (an especially fun and helpful thing to do for epic poetry (*Faerie Queene, Aeneid*, etc.)
- **Context**: If the focus text mentions a person, a piece of art, literature, or music, or a historic event, make a note in the margin and look up the item. Many of the poets, classical music compositions, and artistic works referenced in EIL can be found on the Excellence-in-Literature.com website.
- **Questions**: If you have a question about something in the text, write it in the margin. Writing it down will help you recognize the answer if it later appears in the text. If it does not appear, the written question will remind you to do a bit more research.

If You'd Like To Learn More

If you would like to delve deeper into the structure and analysis of literature, you'll find number of helpful resources in the "Selected Resources" chapter. Adam Andrews' brief *Teaching the Classics* DVD course introduces elements of literature and Socratic discussion using short stories. This course is brief enough to use over the summer before you begin EIL, or even concurrently.

If you are intrigued by the art of reading well, you may also want to read some of the essays on reading that I've mentioned in this chapter (Lewis, Pope, Aristotle) or *How to Read a Book,* Mortimer Adler and Charles Van Doren's classic guide to the art of reading. These resources and others are listed in the resources section at the end of this guide. Enjoy!

Questions to Consider as You Read

If you are not familiar with the terms used in this list, look them up in the Glossary at the back of the guide or in your writer's handbook. These questions may help you think through some of the stories or may be useful in a discussion, but you do not need to spend a lot of time with them.

- Who is the **narrator** of the story, and is he or she reliable or unreliable?
- What types of **conflict** do you see? Possibilities include man vs. man, man vs. God/fate/Providence/the gods, man vs. nature, man vs. society, or even man vs. himself.
- Should [character name] do [whatever he/she is planning]? Why/why not?
- What does it all mean? What great ideas (justice/mercy, friendship, good vs. evil, etc.) seem to be illustrated or embodied in the story?
- Who are the major and minor characters, and what kind of people are they? Consider physical, mental, moral, and spiritual dimensions.
- Do the challenges of the main character reflect common struggles of humanity? Is the character intended to portray an archetype?
- Can you identify the basic stages of the story structure—exposition (background information), rising action (complications), climax, falling action, resolution?
- How is the story told? Possibilities include first-person narrative, a journal, epistolary style (told as a series of letters), etc. How does this method affect your understanding of each of the story elements?
- Does the method of storytelling affect your enjoyment of the plot?
- What symbolism do you see, and how effectively does it enhance your understanding?
- Who or what is the antagonist—whoever or whatever is opposing the protagonist in the conflict?
- What role does each character play in revealing the story?
- What **plot devices** does the author use to move the story along? Possibilities include flashbacks, narrative frames, foreshadowing, genre-specific conventions, and so forth.
- Why has the author used a specific word rather than a synonym in the way and in the place he/she has used it? Would a synonym work as well? Why or why not?

How to Write an Essay

The time to begin writing an article is when you have finished it to your satisfaction. By that time you begin to clearly and logically perceive what it is you really want to say.
—Mark Twain

An essay is a short writing assignment on a particular subject. According to the *Oxford Shorter English Dictionary*, the word *essay* is derived from the Latin root *exigere*, which means to ascertain or weigh. It is also defined as "a first tentative attempt at learning, composition, etc.; a first draft." The essay is sometimes called a position paper, because it must be an expression of the writer's conclusion about a matter, rather than a simple report.

Essays can be written to inform, explain, argue a position, or analyze an issue. Because the writer is expressing an opinion or interpretation, each essay can be seen as an attempt to persuade the reader that your thesis is plausible. Because the essay form involves all steps of the writing process, you will be able to apply the skills learned to any type of writing you do in the future.

In Excellence in Literature, you will have the opportunity to write essays, approach papers, literature summaries, author profiles, and various creative types of writing. The essay prompt in each module will provide an exact subject, and you will find that writing itself will turn into a process of discovery. You will rarely know the answer to the questions in the essay prompt until you begin writing, but as you consider what you have read, you can begin to formulate a thesis. From there, you will be able to write yourself into greater understanding and a reasonable conclusion.

The Writing Process

In the art of classical rhetoric, Cicero outlined five canons—stages or principles for structure or evaluation—for public discourse, especially oration or public speaking. We use three of these canons, Invention, Arrangement, and Style (the remaining two are Memory and Delivery) as guides for written composition. Here's what happens within each part of the process.

- Invention, also called Discovery, is the process of coming up with ideas;
- Arrangement, otherwise known as Disposition, is the process of organizing; placing ideas in the most logical and compelling order;
- Style, sometimes referred to as Elocution, is the process of appropriately and effectively expressing ideas.

This writing process provides a simple outline of what it takes to gather ideas, put them in order, and write them in a way that is understandable and appealing. The kinds of things you will do in each stage are listed and described below. Whatever you are writing—essay, research paper, story, song, poem, whatever—these are the basic things you will do to get yourself from a blank page to a completed project.

1. **Invention**
    - Read/Research
    - Think on Paper
2. **Arrangement**
    - Organize Ideas
3. **Style**
    - Write
    - Revise

Read and Research

To begin an essay assignment, gather information through reading and research. For Excellence in Literature assignments, this means you will read the focus text and assigned context resources, plus any other resources that seem relevant. If you look for additional research materials, be sure they are from reliable sources such as published encyclopedias and reference books, college websites, and original source documents.

Think on Paper with a Mind Map

When you "Think on Paper" in the second step of the writing process, you begin to connect your reading and research with the essay prompt. I use mind mapping to think on paper. This is a quick way to capture ideas and supporting points in an organic form that helps you think freely and creatively. Ideally, mind maps are written by hand, but this example was made with a free web app called Coggle.it.

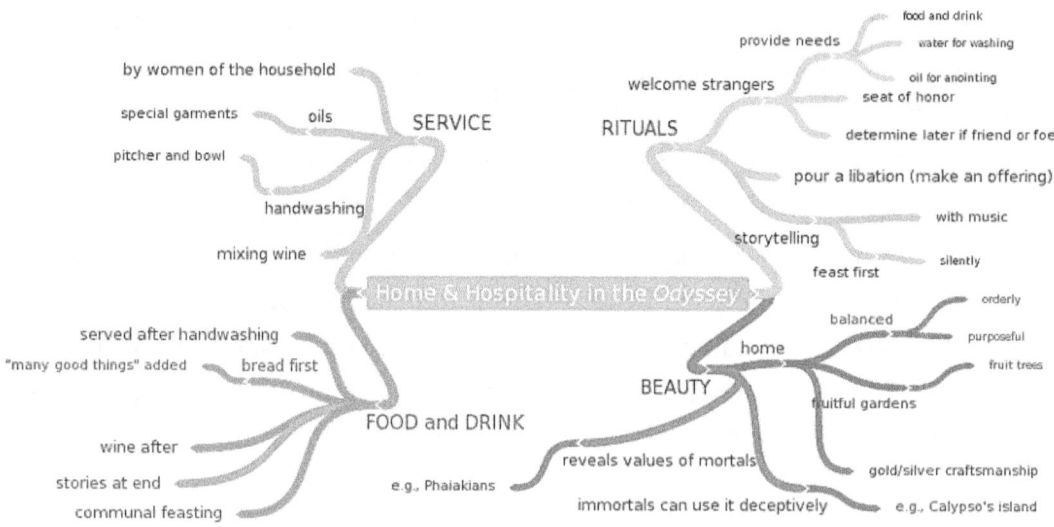

How to Make Your Own Mind Map

1. At the center of your paper, write a few words that summarize the topic or question you are supposed to answer.

2. Draw a line radiating from the center idea for each relevant fact, possible argument, proof point, or supporting detail that comes to mind.

3. Branch off these ideas as additional details emerge.

4. Write down everything that comes to mind, even if you are not sure it fits. Generating ideas is like turning on a faucet for hot water. What comes out at first is not hot, but it has to come out before what you really want can emerge. Your best ideas usually begin to flow after your mind has warmed up and settled into thinking about a topic.

5. Record each idea on the mind map as a word or phrase rather than a complete sentence, and feel free to use symbols and abbreviations to briefly capture your idea.

Additional Mind Mapping Ideas

- You may use color in your mind maps, but it is best not to create an elaborate color coding scheme before you start thinking on paper, as this can be distracting when you're trying to focus on ideas. I usually just add color during the organization stage.

- Some people prefer to use quick sketches rather than words to capture some or all of their ideas. If this is the way your mind works and it does not slow you down too much, feel free to draw.

- Mind maps are usually made with pen or pencil on paper, but you can also use small size sticky notes—one per idea—and make a mind map with those. Do what works for you.

- You can see many examples of mind maps at my Pinterest board for mind maps: pinterest.com/janicecampbell/mind-maps/.

Organize Ideas

Once you have generated several ideas, you must decide which ideas best fit the essay assignment, and how they might logically flow. Group ideas into three categories: Pro/Positive, Con/Negative, and Interesting. Once you have grouped your thoughts into these categories, you will probably have more ideas than you need. Select the most compelling points and interesting examples, and decide how to organize them.

Look at the ordered ideas, and determine whether your thesis will be a Pro/Positive or Con/Negative answer to the essay prompt, or whether you will take an equivocal position in which you provide evidence for and against both sides of the question and leave the reader to decide which perspective seems most compelling.

Thesis Statement

Draft a thesis statement that outlines your position and describes how you will support your argument. In its most elementary form, the thesis can be as simple as a transformation of the essay prompt into a thesis statement.

On the next page, you'll find an example of what it looks like to turn a question—the essay prompt—into a thesis statement. The statement you will craft is similar to what you would write if you were told to answer

---

What is a thesis?

A statement or an opinion that is discussed in a logical way and presented with evidence in order to prove that it is true.

Oxford Learner's Dictionary

a question in a complete sentence. It contains the essence of the question you are answering along with an indication of your answer and sometimes a pointer toward the reason for your example.

Question (adapted from a portion of the essay prompt in *American Literature* Module 2):

- How did the courtship strategies of Irving's characters compare to those of Longfellow's characters?

Question transformed into a thesis statement:

- Although Bram Bones and John Alden were successful in their respective courtships, their courtship strategies differed from one another in several specific ways, including [insert three ways here].

The thesis statement would usually appear near the end of the introductory paragraph, completing the job of orienting the reader to the topic and your position.

Topic Sentence Outline

It can be helpful to transform your list of ideas and supporting points into an essay framework by writing a topic sentence (TS) outline. You are not required to do this for every essay, but I recommend doing it for at least three of the modules in this book. It is simpler and more appropriate for the papers that you'll be writing than a classic alphanumeric outline, which works very well for longer pieces such as a research paper.

In this outline format, topic sentences introduce each supporting paragraph in the body of the essay and announce the proof you will be presenting in that paragraph. Following the topic sentence will be two or more sentences supporting the argument or providing the information found in the topic sentence. Here is an example of a topic sentence outline from the EIL *Handbook for Writers*, which provides detailed instructions for this type of outline:

Sample Outline For a Short Essay on Homer

General Subject: Homer's *Odyssey*

Focus 1: The importance of the home and hospitality

Focus 2: Home and hospitality in *The Odyssey*: the significance of food

Thesis: In *The Odyssey*, the frequent and detailed attention to food and the rituals surrounding it serve constantly to reinforce a central concern of the poem, the vital civilizing importance of the home.

TS 1: Throughout *The Odyssey*, we witness the way in which food taken communally can act as a way of re-energizing human beings, enabling them to cope with their distress. This, in fact, emerges as one of the most important human values in the poem. (Paragraph argues for the restorative values of food as brought out repeatedly in the poem.)

TS 2: The rituals surrounding food, especially the importance of welcoming guests to the feast and making sure everyone has enough, stress the warmth and central importance of open human interaction. (The paragraph argues the importance of hospitality as it is brought out by the references to food and feasting.)

TS 3: The occasions in which food is consumed are also moments in which the participants celebrate the artistic richness of their culture. No where else in the poem is there so much attention paid to the significance of beauty in various forms. (Paragraph X argues that all the things associated with the food—the serving dishes, the entertainment, and so on—reflect important values in the culture.)

Conclusion: There is, of course, much more to the poem than the description of feasting, but we need to recognize these moments as especially important. (Paragraph restates and summarizes the central point of the argument.)

Note: Remain flexible as you write, because it is quite possible to discover another angle or better idea as you are writing. If this happens, do not worry about sticking exactly to your outline. The outline is simply a tool for organization, so you, as the author, are still in charge. Do what works.

Write the Essay

Once you have organized your ideas, it is time to begin writing. At this stage, you have thoroughly thought through the question and your ideas, and have a sturdy framework to build on. Begin writing your first draft, following the general outline you have created.

Type your paper on the computer, following the formatting instructions contained in "Making Your Essay Look Good: The Basics of MLA Format," which is the last example in the **Formats and Models** chapter. At this stage, your primary concerns will be to successfully answer the essay prompt and to support your argument with relevant examples from the text. Look at the rubric in the back of the book to remind yourself of standards goals in the content, style, and mechanics of the paper.

Revise

When the draft is completed, read it aloud to yourself. This will help you pinpoint areas that seem unclear or poorly expressed. Do not skip this step! As you find things that need to be fixed, mark them and keep reading, so you do not lose the flow of the text. When you are finished, go through and fix the things you have marked. When it is as good as you can make it, turn it in.

When you receive the paper back from your writing mentor, read it aloud once again. You may be surprised to notice additional ways in which you can improve it. Refer to the evaluation rubric that you receive along with the essay, and make any improvements recommended there or in your teacher's marginal comments. Focus on fine tuning the style of the paper, including word choice, sentence fluency, and voice. You will find basic standards for these areas listed on the rubric, but your writer's handbook will help you learn even more.

Finally, when you have completed the edits recommended by your teacher, and you feel your essay meets the standards listed on the rubric, read it aloud once more. Change anything that does not sound right, check the mechanics, and when you are satisfied, turn it in.

As you follow this simple, orderly process in assignment after assignment, it will become automatic for you, and writing will become easier. By the time you reach college, you will be able to confidently tackle any writing assignment you encounter. I wish you joy in the craft of writing!

Resources You May Find Helpful
- *Excellence in Literature Handbook for Writers*
- *The Lost Tools of Writing* from the Circe Institute
- *The Elegant Essay Writing Lessons* by Lesha Myers
- *The Mind Map Book* by Tony Buzan
- *Writing to Learn* by William Zinsser

Discerning Worldview through Literary Periods

Every age has its own outlook. It is specially good at seeing certain truths and specially liable to make certain mistakes. We all, therefore, need the books that will correct the characteristic mistakes of our own period. And that means the old books.

—C. S. Lewis

When you are studying literature in context, literary periods can help you understand a bit about the philosophy or worldview that undergirds the literary and artistic fashions of the day. You'll be able to see how the ideas of the Renaissance or the Modern periods are heard in the music of the time; seen in the arts; and embodied in the stories of the period. As you become acquainted with the assumptions that shaped each period, you can understand something about the author's influences before you even read the book.

There are six major periods or movements in English-language literature, and each is described below with its approximate time frame. Each period has sub-periods within it, as well as overlapping characteristics. I have chosen (with permission) to adapt and use the brief system of categories used by Adam Andrews in *Teaching the Classics*. These six major categories give you a very general overview of the period,; you will find greater detail at the Excellence in Literature website, with specific links referenced within the Context Resources. The six periods we will use are:

Medieval (AD 500–1500)   Renaissance (1500–1660)

Neoclassical (1660–1800)   Romantic (1800–1865)

Realist (1840–1914)   Modernist (1900–1945)

Medieval (AD 500–1500)

The **Medieval** period includes the Anglo-Saxon period in the time before the 1066 Norman conquest of England, and the Middle English period after the conquest. **Anglo-Saxon** literature, which is based on oral storytelling, focuses on the heroic ideal which involved responsibility, leadership, loyalty, generosity, and skill in battle. After Christianity reached Britain in the seventh century, literature became overwhelmingly Christian in its themes, while still retaining its concern for the heroic ideal. The epic poem *Beowulf* is a characteristic work from this period.

The **Middle English** period was marked by a change in the purpose and audience for written literature. Anglo-Saxon works had been written by and for the aristocracy, but Middle English literature was by and for people of the lower classes. Rather than the idealized king-heroes of the Anglo-Saxon period, Middle English heroes were everyday people living in everyday situations. Christianity remained central to the medieval world, and most literature reflected this priority. This literary movement roughly coincided with the Gothic period in art and architecture. A well-known work of this period is *The Canterbury Tales* by Geoffrey Chaucer.

Renaissance (1500–1660)

The Renaissance period was a flamboyant, fervent era of exploration and expansion, characterized by several movements, including Renaissance humanism, the Protestant Reformation, Catholic Reformation, and English Nationalism. Renaissance writers were concerned with classical learning, the study of the humanities (language, literature, history, art, and government), the function of religion in the world, and interest in the form and structure of human government. This literary movement roughly coincided with the baroque period in art, music, and architecture.

Authors you will recognize from this period include William Shakespeare, Edmund Spenser, John Donne, and Anne Bradstreet.

Neoclassical (1660–1800)

The Neoclassical period in literature, art, and music roughly coincided with the Age of Enlightenment. Writers in the Neoclassical period favored simplicity, clarity, restraint, regularity, and good sense, as opposed to the intricacy and boldness of the Renaissance period. Neoclassical writers sought to discover meaning in the order of things, placed society before the individual, and viewing humanity as inherently flawed, valued human reason over natural passions. Many of these writers were influenced by the rise of experimental science and the desire for peace and stability. Many sought to imitate the style of Roman writers such as Virgil and Ovid. The art, architecture, and music of this period reflected the aesthetic values of this literary movement.

Writers of this period include Benjamin Franklin, Daniel Defoe, and Jonathan Swift.

Romantic (1800–1865)

Following the French Revolution there was general movement away from the formal literature of the Neoclassical period. Romantic art, music, and literature reflected a belief in mankind's innate goodness, equality, and potential for achievement, and strongly rejected the Neoclassical view of man as a limited being in a strictly hierarchical society. Possibly as a reaction against urbanization and other challenges of the Industrial Revolution, nature was prominently featured as a symbol of freedom of the human soul, and scenic beauty as a model for harmony. Emotion, imagination, and intuition were valued above reason and restraint. This period includes Early and Mid-Victorian literature.

Authors in this tradition include Sir Walter Scott, Mary Shelley, James Fenimore Cooper, and Johann Wolfgang von Goethe.

Realist (1840–1914)

Just as Romantic writers had rejected Neoclassical ideas, Realist authors, artists, and musicians rejected Romantic notions. Realists sought to portray the world and man without idealism, so their works dealt with issues such as industrialization, poverty, and inequality, sometimes focusing on the ugly or sordid. They were interested in the relationship between traditional religion, rationalist thought, and new philosophies such as Darwinism. In England, the Realist period takes place largely during the reign of Queen Victoria (1837–1901), so it includes Mid- and Late Victorian literature.

Realist writers you may know include Charles Dickens, Willa Cather, the Brontë sisters, Booker T. Washington, and Mark Twain.

One form of realism that lasted until World War II was known as **Naturalism**. Influenced by Charles Darwin's theory of evolution, Naturalist writers believed that social conditions, heredity, and environment, rather than Providence or Fate, determined man's destiny, and they often wrote about those on the fringe of society, including the uncouth and sordid. If Romantics saw the individual as a god and Realists saw him as a common man, Naturalists saw him as a helpless animal for whom free will was only an illusion. Naturalist writers include Jack London and Stephen Crane.

Modernist (1900–1945)

The dramatic changes wrought by the Industrial Revolution, Marxism, and modern scientific theories and political developments rocked the faith of twentieth-century writers. At the heart of Modernist literature is a reflection of their conviction that all the traditional structures of human life—religious, social, political, economic, and artistic—had either been destroyed or proven false. The writers' disorientation and uncertainty is often seen in the fragmented form of their fiction, and their protagonists are often aimless and frustrated rather than heroic.

Modernist authors include F. Scott Fitzgerald, Gertrude Stein, T. S. Eliot, Ernest Hemingway, and Ezra Pound.

After World War II, the Modernist movement split into fragments such as Post-Modernism, Imagism, the Harlem Renaissance, Surrealism, Beat poets, Post-colonialists, and others. It is not clear which, if any, of these will prove dominant in historic hindsight. What is certain is that each of the literary periods explored here will help you understand the literature you read, in the context in which it was created.

This summary of literary periods is adapted from Teaching the Classics, *and is used courtesy of Adam Andrews, www.CenterForLit.com.*

If you'd like to know more about worldview, please see the "What is a Worldview?" explanation by Dr. Kenneth H. Funk II, available from the Excellence-in-Literature.com website.

Tips for Using EIL in a Classroom

Words are a lens to focus one's mind.

-Ayn Rand

Teachers are using this curriculum in so many creative ways in classrooms and co-ops everywhere. Eventually, I hope to establish a spot on Excellence-in-Literature.com or our Facebook page for teachers to exchange ideas and find support, but until then, here are few suggestions for using EIL with a group.

First, remember that one of the key features of EIL is the practice of college-level learning skills in addition to literary analysis. C. S. Lewis writes that "Ideally, we should like to define a good book as one which 'permits, invites, or compels' good reading. but we shall have to make do with 'permits and invites'" (*An Experiment in Criticism*, 113). The books in EIL are the kind that permit and invite good reading to those with a receptive ear. Good literary discussions can encourage deeper reading and more thoughtful written responses, so they can be a great benefit even if the discussion takes place in a very small group.

To encourage participation, students should prepare for discussions by doing all the assigned readings before class time. For small groups, each student can be assigned to make a short presentation on a chapter, a portion of the context resources, or on a specific discussion question. The teacher or co-op leader should function as a facilitator, assigning areas of research and guiding discussions, rather than doing the research and lecturing on findings.

As Charlotte Mason admonished, "We err when we allow our admirable teaching to intervene between children and the knowledge their minds demand. The desire for knowledge (curiosity) is the chief agent in education: but this desire may be made powerless like an unused limb" (*A Philosophy of Education*, p. 247). She asks, "What if the devitalisation we notice in so many of our young people, keen about games but dead to things of the mind, is due to the processes carried on in our schools, to our plausible and pleasant ways of picturing, eliciting, demonstrating, illustrating, summarising, doing all those things for children which they are born with the potency to do for themselves?" (p. 237). Simply stated, learning happens when students interact with literature, not when they listen passively to a lecture.

Here are a few ideas for creating an active group learning environment:

- Introduce each module by pointing the student to the Module Focus, Literary Context, and Introduction in the text.
- Assign a context area to each student or group of students, and have them report their findings to the class.
- If the Focus Text is a poem, encourage students to listen to at least a portion of it in a professionally recorded audio version. A poem is meant to be heard, and listening will bring it to life as nothing else can.
- For each module, have students choose one passage or poem to recite or copy by hand. Recitation and copywork both aid retention of ideas and build writing skills, as both require close attention to the use of words and sequence of ideas.
- If the Focus Text is a play, always try to watch the video version. It may be best to watch it after the focus text has been read, so students will be able to appreciate subtle twists and nuances they may otherwise miss.
- Use the *Something to Think About* and *Be Sure to Notice* items as discussion starters after students have begun reading the text.
- Pull a few of the "Questions to Consider as you Read" for discussions. The most fruitful questions tend to be those that evoke an opinionated response:
  - Should [character name] do [whatever he/she is planning]? Why or why not?
  - What does it all mean? What great ideas (justice/mercy, friendship, good vs. evil, etc.) seem to be illustrated or embodied in the story?

- What can you learn, or what do you think the author believes you should do or not do?

- Encourage additional research or sharing of context items not found in the EIL guide. If students find a resource they particularly like, they are welcome to submit it to me at Janice@EverydayEducation.com for possible inclusion in the next edition of EIL.

- When students do an approach paper, choose some of their discussion questions to spark discussions in class. If students have chosen different key passages (this is perfectly fine), encourage them to discuss why they chose the passage they did, and why it is a key.

- When students have finished the focus text, encourage discussion of how it exemplifies its literary period, and ways it may have differed from student expectations.

- If you choose to watch the movie version of a novel as part of the class, discuss how it differs from the author's creation.

- Encourage comparison of the current focus text with other works the student has read in or out of class. As they learn to discern common themes, you may find them referencing *Les Misérables*, *Merchant of Venice*, *The Little Red Hen*, and *The Lion, the Witch and the Wardrobe* in discussions of justice and mercy, love and duty. This means they are seeing *through* each story into the broader story beyond, which is a sign that they are reading deeply and well.

- If you have five classroom periods each week, use one to practice what my high school used to call USSR—Uninterrupted, Sustained, Silent Reading. Many students have never been required to sit quietly for an hour and do anything, but this is an essential skill that needs to be learned, and USSR is a good way to begin. (For more on brain development and the effect of technology on language skills, I recommend *Endangered Minds* and *Failure to Connect* by Dr. Jane Healy.)

Comprehension Questions

I do not believe in using "comprehension questions" at all, except in a very limited way as practice for necessary standardized testing. I do not believe they are useful or effective, especially for high school students who should be learning to love literature, think deeply, and write thoughtfully about the literature they read.

Comprehension questions are often trivia questions which test only student memory or the ability to catch details. Instead of helping students think deeply about the text as a whole, comprehension questions often make reading nothing more than a treasure hunt for answers. I have seen "how to study" guides that suggest students should read the comprehension questions first, then hunt for answers as they skim the story. This may be an effective strategy for timed standardized tests and may seem to be a quick and easy way to finish an assignment and move on, but it completely short circuits the learning process. Plus, it is a fast way to ruin a great book.

The writing prompts provided in EIL encourage students to thoughtfully and analytically consider something specific about the text. It is impossible to write a coherent, thoughtful paper without comprehending what you have read, so it provides a much better measure of how much the student understands about the literary work, and how well he or she writes.

Module 5.1

Odyssey by Homer (c. 7th–9th century BC)

Among all men on the earth bards have a share of honor and reverence,
because the muse has taught them songs and loves the race of bards.

—Homer, *Odyssey* 8. 457 ff

Focus Text

The Odyssey by Homer, translated by Robert Fagles or Richard Lattimore

I strongly recommend that you also listen to a professionally produced audiobook version of this epic poem.

Honors Texts

The Iliad by Homer

Literature Type

Ancient Greek Epic

Module Focus

We will look at the conventions of epic poetry, and the concept of the heroic ideal in Greek literature, and the value of honor and of cunning in *The Odyssey*.

Introduction

In *The Odyssey*, three story lines capture the reader's attention and keep the action moving. In the first, Odysseus seeks to return home after a ten-year absence following the Trojan War. The second story-line deals with Odysseus' faithful wife

Penelope, who efficiently wards off suitors and maintains the estate in Odysseus' absence. Finally, a third story line follows the goddess Athena as she helps Odysseus in his quest to return home. The twenty-four books of the poem can be roughly grouped in four divisions:

- The adventures of Telemachus
- Odysseus' homecoming
- The story of Odysseus' wanderings
- Odysseus on Ithaca

The Odyssey is an epic poem, intended to be heard rather than read, so be sure to listen to at least part of it. As you read, you might want to consider contrasts between the mythological gods of the Greeks, the God of the Hebrew people, and other deities or idols that you are aware of.

Something to think about . . .

The Iliad is a companion tale to the Odyssey. It tells of some of the events of the Trojan War. Its 24 books are considered tragedy, in contrast with the 24 books of *The Odyssey*, which take place over many years and are considered comedy (in the literary sense). When you are finished with the book, think about the literary definition of "comedy" and ways in which *The Odyssey* fits that definition. As you read or listened to it, did you catch the various elements that made it comedic?

Be sure to notice . . .

Epic Characteristics:

- Long narrative poem (tells a story)
- Vast setting develops episodes important to history of a nation, state, people.
- Didactic, giving lessons on appropriate action for the audience
- Great deeds by a hero of mythical, legendary, or historical significance; a person of heroic proportions, high position
- Supernatural forces intervene.
- Elevated style, reflected in formal speeches by main characters

Epic Conventions:

- Poet states theme at opening.
- Invokes muse

- Begins in *medias res*—exposition comes later.
- Catalogues of warriors, ships, armies, weapons
- Extended formal speeches
- Frequent use of formal and sustained epic similes (extended comparison using figurative language)

Context Resources

Readings

Why read *The Odyssey*? Teacher Deborah Stokol's letter to her students offers an interesting view of why you should read it and what you will gain. I recommend starting your context readings here.

https://excellence-in-literature.com/why-read-the-odyssey-2/

In a similar vein, classical educator Cheryl Lowe addresses the question of "Why Study the Pagans"?

https://excellence-in-literature.com/why-study-the-pagans-by-cheryl-lowe/

Professor Chis Mackie has provided brief, nicely illustrated overview of Homer's *Odyssey*. This isn't a substitute for reading the poem, but it can help you understand it.

https://excellence-in-literature.com/guide-to-the-classics-homers-odyssey/

If you find *The Odyssey* a bit intimidating, you may want to start by reading Charles Lamb's children's version, *Tales of Odysseus*.

https://excellence-in-literature.com/the-adventures-of-ulysses-by-charles-lamb/

Another version of *The Odyssey* for young readers is *The Wanderings of Odysseus* by Rosemary Sutcliff. You may also find it useful to read *Black Ships Before Troy*, her retelling of *The Iliad*. Sutcliff is an outstanding writer, and her books bring the historical period to life, especially when combined with the vivid illustrations of artist Alan Lee.

Homer used figures of speech that are now known as Homeric epithets. These included descriptive terms such as "wine-dark sea," "rosy-fingered dawn," and "softly-braided nymph." Some modern writers, including poet W. H. Auden and novelist Thomas Wolfe, have incorporated Homeric epithets into their own writing. The article below is hosted on the digital library, JSTOR, which can often be accessed through your local community or college library.

http://www.jstor.org/pss/3291715

View a timeline of ancient literature from Greek alphabetic scripts in the late 8th-century BC to Matthew and the Gospels around AD 80.

https://wwnorton.com/college/english/nawest/content/timeline/ancient.htm

Tufts University hosts Perseus, a respected site at which you can view Homeric texts in Greek and see a variety of art and architecture illustrations. Scroll down to view Homer's works in both Greek and English, and be sure to view at least three items from the art and architecture section.

http://www.perseus.tufts.edu/hopper/collections

The Author's Life and Historical Context

Very little is known about Homer, but he is thought to have been a blind poet who lived around 700–800 BC. This excellent University of Cincinnati website offers a helpful introduction to the question, "Who was Homer?" Don't hesitate to explore other pages on this fascinating site to learn more about Troy and the Trojan war.

http://cerhas.uc.edu/troy/q402.html

In this Hidden Histories article, you'll discover how archaeology is helping to uncover more about Homer's world, including Troy.

https://excellence-in-literature.com/hidden-histories-by-jonathan-gottschall/

The Archaeological Site of Troy is one of UNESCO's World Heritage Sites. You can see pictures, look at a map, and read more about it at the UNESCO site.

https://whc.unesco.org/en/list/849/

This interesting article considers how it's possible that a "tiny, dirty Greek city-state produced more brilliant minds—from Socrates to Aristotle—" than any place before or since.

https://www.theatlantic.com/science/archive/2016/02/what-made-ancient-athens-a-city-of-genius/462009/

For a look at other historical events from Homer's time, you may want to read I and II Kings in any translation of the Bible.

This interview with *Iliad* and *Odyssey* translator Robert Fagles will give you an idea of what goes into translation, as well as additional insight into Homer's work.

https://www.c-span.org/video/?95780-1/odyssey-iliad-translations

How do epics like the *Iliad* and *Odyssey* survive the centuries? Just imagine—these stories were being told about 700 years before the time of Jesus; about 300 years before Plato; and about sixteen centuries before *Beowulf*. In this online exhibit from the University of Chicago, you can read about the stories' history and see some of the early manuscripts, including one on a papyrus fragment.

https://www.lib.uchicago.edu/collex/exhibits/homer-print-transmission-and-reception-homers-works/homer-print/

Poetry

The Odyssey, like many other great works, has inspired works of art, music, and literature, including the following poems:

"Ithaka" by C. P. Cavafy speaks of the concept of Odysseus' long journey toward home, as well as the true meaning of home.

https://www.ithaca.org.au/about-ithaca/poem-from-cavafy

"Odysseus to Telemachus" by Joseph Brodsky is written as a letter from an aging, absent father to his growing son.

https://poets.org/poem/odysseus-telemachus

"Ode On a Grecian Urn" by John Keats speaks of the beauty and symbolism of a Grecian urn. When you read this, be sure to look at the images referenced in the Visual Arts section so that you understand Keats' imagery.

https://excellence-in-literature.com/ode-on-a-grecian-urn-by-john-keats

This study guide may help you understand this poem:

http://www.cummingsstudyguides.net/Guides2/Keats.html

One of my favorite poems is "On First Looking into Chapman's Homer." When poet John Keats received Chapman's new translation of Homer's work, he and a friend were so excited about it that they sat up all night reading it. Keats wrote this poem the next morning.

https://excellence-in-literature.com/upon-first-looking-upon-chapmans-homer-by-john-keats

https://excellence-in-literature.com/melani-study-guide-on-first-looking-into-chapmans-homer/

Audio

Listen to the Robert Fagles translation as an audio book performed by Ian McKellen. You can get it on CD from Amazon.com, as a download from Audible.com, or as a cassette tape from AudioBooksOnline.com.

The entire poem is available as a free audio download, but this is not the best way to listen to it, as the translation is not as good, and the reading is done by a variety of amateurs with mixed results. Only use this if you absolutely cannot get a professionally-produced audiobook.

http://librivox.org/the-odyssey-by-homer

Music

At this composer's site, you can listen to the music and read a bit of the history of the lyre. At the links below you will see ancient lyres similar to those that might have been used by Homer and other ancients, including King David, the Psalmist.

https://ancientlyre.com/lyres-of-the-ancient-world

https://ancientlyre.com/historical-research

https://excellence-in-literature.com/ancient-greek-music-macedonia/

Here is an interesting overview of ancient Greek instruments:

http://www.homoecumenicus.com/ancient_instruments.htm

Listen to a brief audio sample of "Calypso and Ulysses" as it may have originally been sung, and read the original Greek text and its English translation.

http://homoecumenicus.com/ioannidis_homer_odyssey.htm

Video

The Odyssey was filmed as a TV movie in 1997, but I have not seen it, so cannot judge whether it is suitable for family viewing. According to one review, it is "absorbing and believable," and a second commenter recommends it, saying that he/she watched it in a ninth-grade class.

https://www.imdb.com/title/tt0118414/

Visual Arts

The Metropolitan Museum of Art's *Heilbrun Timeline of Art History* offers excellent images, including photos of several urns and detailed, interesting information on "The Art of Classical Greece" (ca. 480–323 BC) Click on images to enlarge them.

https://www.metmuseum.org/toah/hd/tacg/hd_tacg.htm

You may view "Scenes from the *Odyssey* in Ancient Art" in the slideshow on this page at Oxford University Press.

https://blog.oup.com/2014/07/scenes-from-the-odyssey-in-ancient-art/

This University of Pennsylvania website features an interactive map of Odysseus' journey.

https://www2.classics.upenn.edu/myth/content/homer/multimap.html

Classics professor Walter Englert of Reed College offers several resources for understanding the *Iliad*, including a map, timeline, outline, art, and more.

https://www.reed.edu/humanities/110Tech/Iliad.html#HomericGeography

Ancient Greece (DK Eyewitness Books) by Anne Pearson offers beautiful maps, photos of Greek architecture, mosaics, weapons, armor, jewelry, and much more. You can most likely find this at your local library.

Just for Fun

If you are studying *The Odyssey* in a class or co-op, you may enjoy playing the Trojan War game.

http://www.mythologyteacher.com/Trojan-War-Game.php

In *Argos*, author Ralph Hardy has retold the story of the *Odyssey* through the voice and personality of Argos, Odysseus's old dog who was waiting for his master to come home. This interview with Hardy might make you want to read the book!

https://www.pbs.org/video/nc-bookwatch-ralph-hardy-argos/

At the *Norton Anthology* site, you can take a quiz on the *Odyssey* and other classic works. This is not required, but it can be fun to test your knowledge.

https://wwnorton.com/college/english/nawest/content/quiz/reading/ancient.htm

Here are two crossword puzzles based on the *Odyssey*—the first is fairly simple; the second a little more complex:

https://www.armoredpenguin.com/crossword/Data/best/literature/odyssey.04.html

http://www.groseducationalmedia.ca/greekm/ody.html

Vocabulary

Here is a guide to the some of the unusual vocabulary you will encounter in *The Odyssey*. It's also a good idea to keep your own personal list of characters and events so that you can keep track of who's who as you read or listen.

https://www.vocabulary.com/lists/85024

Assignment Schedule

Week 1

Begin reading the context resources and listening to or reading the epic. You may wish to begin by reading Charles Lamb's version or a summary; then move into the full version of the *Odyssey*. As you finish each of the twenty-four books, write a brief (five sentences or fewer) summary of its events. If you prefer, you may create a sketch of the major scenes in each book. This will help you find specific sections as you are writing your essay.

Week 2

When you finish the poem, write a historical approach paper on Ancient Greece. You will find the format and a sample paper in the Formats and Models chapter. In addition to the context links I have provided, you may use other resources such as your encyclopedia, the library, and quality Internet resources to complete this assignment.

Week 3

Begin drafting a 750-word paper on one of the topics below. I recommend that you follow the writing process outlined in the "How to Write an Essay" chapter, consulting the models in the Formats and Models chapter and your writer's handbook as needed.

1) Model: Literary Analysis Essay and MLA Format Model

Prompt: Although *The Odyssey* is written from a pagan worldview and features mythical creatures, including beings described as gods and goddesses, the poem praises virtues such as honor, justice, respect for elders, hospitality to strangers, and fidelity to marriage and to duty. Choose one of these virtues, and draft a 750-page paper discussing ways in which Homer illustrates this virtue and its results through his characters' lives. You may compare and contrast Homer's portrayal of these virtues with a Biblical or modern example of the same virtue if you wish. Be sure to use quotes from the text to support your thesis.

2) Model: A chapter in *The Odyssey* and MLA Format Model

Prompt: Using the brief book-by-book summary you created in the first weeks of this module as a guide, focus on the story of Telemachus, Penelope, or Odysseus, to retell the story with a modern setting and characters. Be sure to maintain the balanced tone and pacing of the original version. Remember that mythical characters play a substantial role in this classic quest tale, so you may choose to use them in your retelling, as well. Your story should be at least 750 words, and may be as long as necessary to tell a good story.

Turn in the draft at the end of the week, so your writing mentor can evaluate it using the Content standards (Ideas/Concepts and Organization) on the rubric.

Week 4

Use the feedback on the rubric along with the writing mentor's comments to revise your paper. Before turning in the final draft, be sure you have addressed any issues marked on the evaluation rubric, and verify that the thesis is clear and your essay is well-organized. Use your writer's handbook to check grammar or punctuation so that your essay will be free from mechanical errors. Turn in the essay at the end of the week so that the writing mentor can use the evaluation rubric in the "How to Evaluate" chapter to check your work.

Module 5.2

Antigone by Sophocles (496–406 BC)

In the end it is the ancient codes—oh my regrets! That one must keep:
to value life then one must value law.

—*Antigone*, Lines 1237

Focus Text

Antigone by Sophocles (Use a good annotated version, or this module will be challenging. I like the notes found in the *Norton Anthology of World Literature*, which your library may have, and the Robert Fagles translation is excellent.)

The Burial at Thebes: A Version of Sophocles' Antigone by Seamus Heaney: Irish poet Seamus Heaney offers an immensely approachable version of *Antigone*. Be sure to read at least some of it aloud.

Here is an online translation of *Antigone*, followed by a brief commentary:

http://www.perseus.tufts.edu/hopper/text?doc=Perseus:text:1999.01.0186

http://www.perseus.tufts.edu/hopper/text?doc=Perseus:text:1999.04.0023

Honors Text

Oedipus Rex by Sophocles

Literary Period

Greek Tragedy

Module Focus

We will consider the elements of tragedy and observe how the structure of Greek drama and use of the chorus affects the impact of the play.

Note: The name "Antigone" is pronounced with four syllables: an **ti** guh nee.

Introduction

Sophocles' plays are outstanding examples of tragedy (review the definition in the glossary to be sure you understand it), and they remain thought provoking after hundreds of years because they raise timeless questions about how to live life. People continue to grapple with questions of authority and duty, and pride is an ever-present stumbling block for those in leadership. As you read through *Antigone,* think about these issues, and consider how the play helps you reach a conclusion.

Something to think about . . .

Consider the questions facing Antigone, Ismene, and Creon. Can you think of a similar situation that might arise today? Are there easy answers? Would the story have been as memorable if it had ended happily?

Be sure to notice . . .

There is a formal stylistic interplay between the dialog of the characters and the chorus. What is the function of the chorus in the play?

Context Resources

Readings

"The Classics Pages" by Andrew Wilson offers a brief introduction to various aspects of the play. Begin at the link below, and read the introductory page and the following pages: "How old was Antigone?"; "The Character of Creon—persuasion and getting persuaded"; and "Ismene—how should she be portrayed?".

http://www.users.globalnet.co.uk/~loxias/antigone.htm

The ancient Greeks were famous for using formal rhetorical devices to make their speech and writing more powerful. Retired English professor Robert Harris has written a handy guide to sixty of the traditional devices. They are well worth studying.

http://www.virtualsalt.com/a-handbook-of-rhetorical-devices/

Dr. Robin Mitchell-Boyask of Temple University has put together an excellent study guide for *Antigone*. You may wish to print this out, and think of the questions it poses as you read through the play.

https://jan.ucc.nau.edu/jgr6/201%20web/unit11/study_guide_antigone.htm

Read about the structure of a hero's journey. How does Antigone's story fit this model?

https://excellence-in-literature.com/heros-journey/

Here is a glossary of terms used in Greek tragedy, plus an *Antigone*-specific list:

http://www.temple.edu/classics/dramaterms/index.html

https://www.vocabulary.com/lists/267676

Here is a helpful 1906 overview and analysis of the play:

http://www.theatrehistory.com/ancient/bates017.html

The Author's Life

In the *Norton Anthology of World Literature* (or in the introduction of another good annotated version of the story), read the mini-biography of Sophocles and the overview of *Antigone*.

Sophocles is analyzed as a dramatist in this helpful overview, reprinted from a 1906 book, *The Drama: Its History, Literature and Influence on Civilization*.

http://www.theatrehistory.com/ancient/sophocles001.html

Use your encyclopedia or the online sources below to read more about Sophocles and his influence on drama.

https://www.notablebiographies.com/Sc-St/Sophocles.html

http://www.imagi-nation.com/moonstruck/clsc1.htm

Poetry

Read the excerpt of the Seamus Heaney translation of *Antigone* that was reprinted in *The Guardian*. Does the poetic nature of this translation seem to fit the story? Which translation (the one in your book or the Heaney one) seems clearer and/or more interesting?

https://www.theguardian.com/books/2004/feb/21/poetry.seamusheaney

Sophocles' poetry has been translated many times. You may read "Prayer for Deliverance from the Pestilence" and other selections at the links below.

https://www.poetry-archive.com/s/prayer_for_deliverance.html

https://www.poetry-archive.com/s/long_life_not_to_be_desired.html

William Butler Yeats reflected poetically on *Antigone* in "From *The Antigone*."

https://www.poemhunter.com/poem/from-the-antigone/

Audio

Be sure to listen to at least part of *Antigone* in audio format. Remember, it is a drama, and was written to be performed, rather than read.

Professionally recorded audio: http://audible.com

Free, amateur audio: http://librivox.org/antigone-by-sophocles/

Music

Composer Felix Mendelssohn created incidental music for *Antigone*. His composition, *Antigone, Op. 55*, is one of his lesser-known scores but is available on CD. You may read about it at the link below and listen to it at bottom of the Resources page linked below.

https://excellence-in-literature.com/ancient-greek-literature-resources-index/

These reviews of Mendelssohn's beautiful composition will help you understand its purpose and form.

https://www.gramophone.co.uk/review/mendelssohn-antigone

http://www.musicweb-international.com/classrev/2009/Oct09/Mendelssohn_antigone_83224.htm

Video

National Theatre, UK, offers a brief video introduction to the art of Greek tragedy.

https://excellence-in-literature.com/greek-tragedy-an-introduction/

I have not seen the 1961 Greek film of *Antigoni* (with English subtitles), but it was well-reviewed and may be a helpful addition to this module.

https://www.imdb.com/title/tt0055375/

There is also a 1974 *Antigone* (Broadway Theatre Archive) available on DVD.

How can Antigone be presented as a contemporary drama? Here's one answer from the British National Theatre:

https://excellence-in-literature.com/antigone-video-introduction/

Visual Arts

Antigone was depicted as a tragic heroine by Victorian painter Frederic Leighton.

https://excellence-in-literature.com/ancient-greek-literature-in-art/ (Scroll down.)

Polish artist Antoni Brodowski painted *Oedipus and Antigone* in 1828.

http://artyzm.com/e_obraz.php?id=602

If you have an art history book or can get one from your local library, look at the section on art from ancient Greece. This will give you more insight into what the people of this era found beautiful.

Historic Context

Eyewitness Ancient Greece by Anne Pearson offers an excellent visual overview of Ancient Greek culture. It should be available at your local library.

If you have a timeline of the ancient world in an encyclopedia or history book, take a look at what was happening in the world around the time of Sophocles. What other writers or art works may have affected him or his worldview?

https://wwnorton.com/college/history/ralph/referenc/wrldtime.htm

Retired university professor, Ian Johnston, provides a thorough introduction to classical Greek literature.

https://excellence-in-literature.com/
some-preliminary-observations-on-classical-greek-literature-by-ian-johnston/

Assignment Schedule

Week 1

Read and explore context materials, and begin reading focus text. Follow the model in the Formats and Models chapter to write an Author Profile. Be sure to refer to your writer's handbook if you have questions about grammar, structure, or style.

You may find it helpful to use study questions as you think through the text, though you must not get distracted from the story by the questions (if you find them distracting while you are reading, just look them over before and after). You do not need to write answers for them.

You will find a downloadable set of study questions from teacher Amy Allison's website at the first link below—just click on "Oxford Study Guide" to download this excellent resource from Oxford World Classics. A second study guide is available from Dr. Robin Mitchell-Boyask of Temple University.

http://www.temple.edu/classics/antigone/index.html

http://www.scasd.org/Page/13418 (Click on "Oxford Study Guide.")

Week 2

Write an approach paper, using the instructions and samples in the Formats and Models chapter. In addition to the context links I have provided, you may use other resources such as your encyclopedia, the library, and quality Internet resources to help you complete this assignment.

Week 3

Begin drafting a 750-word paper on the topic below. I recommend that you follow the writing process outlined in the "How to Write an Essay" chapter, consulting the models in the Formats and Models chapter and your writer's handbook as needed.

Model: Literary Analysis Essay and MLA Format Model

Prompt: *Antigone* is a story of many "no" answers. Who are the "no"-sayers, and what is the result of their "no" in the development of the story? Which of the people who said "no" were able to stick with their original answer, and how did this affect the outcome of the story? How did the many "no" answers affect the mood of the play? Be sure to support your thesis with appropriate quotes from the text and your research.

Alternate Assignment

Rewrite the story in prose or poetry. Tell the story with colorful details, making sure that your reader will finish the tale with a vivid understanding of the characters and events. Make this at least 750 words or as long as necessary in order to tell a good tale.

Turn in the draft at the end of the week, so your writing mentor can evaluate it using the Content standards (Ideas/Concepts and Organization) on the rubric.

Week 4

Use the feedback on the rubric, along with the writing mentor's comments to revise your paper. Before turning in the final draft, be sure you have addressed any issues marked on the evaluation rubric, and verify that the thesis is clear and your essay is well-organized. Use your writer's handbook to check grammar or punctuation so that your essay will be free from mechanical errors. Turn in the essay at the end of the week so that the writing mentor can use the evaluation rubric in the "How to Evaluate" chapter to check your work.

Module 5.3

The Aeneid by Virgil (70–19 BC)

Remember by your strength to rule Earth's peoples—for your arts are to be these:
to pacify, to impose the rule of law, to spare the conquered, battle down the proud.

—Virgil's "Roman Mandate" (VI.1151–1154)

Focus Text

The Aeneid (c. 30-21 BC) by Publius Vergilius Maro (better known as Virgil or Vergil)

This epic poem tells the story of the origins of Rome. I recommend the translations by Robert Fitzgerald or Robert Fagles. To decide which one to use, visit Amazon.com and click on the book cover to look inside. You will be able to read the first page of each, which will give you a sense of each author's style. These are both excellent translations with good annotations, so choose the one you like (my personal copy is the Fitzgerald translation, which is also used in the Norton Anthology).

To keep track of events as you are reading, you may use this book outline by college professor William Johnson from the University of Cincinnati. Summaries from John Dryden's translation are included.

http://excellence-in-literature.com/world-lit/e5-resources/aeneid-study-guide-by-william-johnson

Honors Text

Lives of the Noble Grecians and Romans by Plutarch: Read at least six of the parallel life stories, choosing the ones that interest you most. You can find it at libraries or bookstores. Here is an online version at the University of Chicago:

https://penelope.uchicago.edu/Thayer/E/Roman/Texts/Plutarch/Lives/home.html

Literary Period

Ancient Rome

Module Focus

In this module, we will observe differences between *The Odyssey* and *The Aeneid*, and consider how they relate to the differences between Greek and Roman society and values.

Introduction

In *The Aeneid*, Virgil recorded an enduring legend of how the survivors of the Trojan War fought their way to a new land and settled the area that became Rome. He is one of the few writers who did not fall out of favor in the West, and his masterwork, *The Aeneid*, has been studied by generation after generation.

Using the form of an epic poem, he tells a story that has almost become the history of Rome. Virgil was chosen for the task of writing this epic by Caesar Augustus, and he spent the last eleven years of his life working on it. Virgil and *The Aeneid* had such an impact on the Italian poet Dante Alighieri that he included Virgil in his own great work, *The Divine Comedy*, as his guide to the underworld.

Something to think about . . .

According to scholars, the political ideas and institutions of the United States of America are heavily influenced by Virgil's *Aeneid*. Most of our founding fathers were students of the classics, and they studied them deeply, usually in the original language. As you read through *The Aeneid*, watch for ideas that may have influenced the U. S. Constitution and Bill of Rights.

Be sure to notice . . .

Unlike *The Iliad* and *The Odyssey*, to which it is often compared, *The Aeneid* was a literary epic. This means that it was originally written, rather than spoken, so it tends to be more tightly structured. Like *The Iliad* and *The Odyssey*, it is structured in a poetic meter known as dactylic hexameter (look in your writer's handbook or search online for "define: dactylic hexameter" for a detailed explanation).

Context Resources

Readings

In Search of a Homeland by Penelope Lively retells the story of *The Aeneid* for younger readers. It is an excellent introduction to the full-length adult version, so I recommend reading it first. (https://amzn.to/3axfiYl)

The University of Pennsylvania has created an online version of *The Aeneid*, linked to a concordance and other reference materials. Look at the "About the Vergil Project" link for instructions on how to use the site.

http://vergil.classics.upenn.edu

Dr. William A. Johnson, a professor of Classical Studies at Duke University, has created an excellent study guide for The Aeneid. You'll find this very helpful as you read or listen through the poem.

https://excellence-in-literature.com/aeneid-study-guide-by-william-johnson/

The Author's Life

Read about Virgil in an encyclopedia, *Norton Anthology of World Literature*, or other resource.

This brief online biography was written by the Roman historian Suetonius, who lived from about AD 69–75 to sometime after 130.

https://excellence-in-literature.com/virgil-biography

Poetry

Like modern poetry, Roman poetry features a wide variety of forms, including epigrams and elegies. Here are examples from poets Martial and Catullus.

https://excellence-in-literature.com/roman-poetry/

Satire I is the first poem in *The Satires*, a collection of satirical poems written by the Roman poet Horace around 33-35 BC. It's a bit longer, and more conversational in tone, with a focus on the question of human happiness.

https://excellence-in-literature.com/satire-i-by-horace

Roman Poetry: From the Republic to the Silver Age by Dorothea Wender- This charming little volume contains mini-biographies and poems by Catullus, Lucretius, Virgil, Horace, Propertius, Tibullus, Ovid, Martial, and Juvenal. Look for it at your local library or a university library, or you can read part of it at Google Books (just type the title into the search box on the home page below).

http://books.google.com

The Society For The Oral Reading Of Greek And Latin Literature (SORGLL) offers an audio reading of Horace's *Ode 1.22*. You can read along with the translated text. Notice the things the poet seems to value. You'll also find these audio readings toward the bottom of our EIL "Roman Poetry" page.

https://soundcloud.com/rhapsodoi/sets/latin-recordings

Roman Myth

Ovid (Publius Ovidius Naso c. 43 BC – AD 17/18) is a Roman writer of the Augustan age. He is best known as a poet and the author of the *Metamorphoses*, in which the Echo and Narcissus myth first appeared.

http://excellence-in-literature.com/world-lit/e5-resources/echo-and-narcissus-by-ovid

Audio

Because this is an epic poem, it will be very helpful to listen to at least part of it rather than simply reading it. Here's a link to a good audiobook version narrated by Frederick Davidson.

http://amzn.to/2qhEVmM

Listen to at least a portion of both of the readings in Latin from Vergil's *Aeneid*. Notice the lyrical sound of the poem as the narrators read expressively. Which of the two readings evokes the sound of lamentation?

https://excellence-in-literature.com/roman-poetry/

Your library may offer a professional audio recording of *Aeneid*, but if not, Librivox offers a free audio version of the Dryden translation.

http://librivox.org/aeneid-by-vergil/

Music

The Trojans or *Les Troyens* is a French opera based on the story of Troy from Virgil's epic poem *The Aeneid*. Written between 1856 and 1858 by composer Hector Berlioz, it debuted in Paris on 4 November 1863. You may listen to at least a bit of *Les Troyens,* at the first link and read a brief synopsis of it by the Metropolitan Opera at the second. If you like the opera, you'll find another good performance at the third link. As you listen to it and read the synopsis, notice what was kept in and what was left out.

https://youtu.be/JVuj-bozXVE

https://www.metopera.org/user-information/synopses-archive/les-troyens

https://amzn.to/32BFMTY

Video

The Avenger: The Legend of The Aeneid (1962) may be available from your library or online streaming service. I have not watched the entire movie, so I cannot attest to its quality.

Ancient Rome grew from a small town into a mighty empire that dominated most of Europe, Britain, and parts of Asia, Africa, and the Mediterranean islands for centuries. They built viaducts to carry water, roadways that are still in use, and many other things including special types of weapons. These videos will introduce you to some of the weapons and their uses.

https://excellence-in-literature.com/roman-weapons-video/

https://excellence-in-literature.com/roman-water-wheel-london-museum/

Visual Arts

If you have an art history book, look at the Roman art and architecture depicted there. Notice ways in which it differs from Greek art and architecture. Remember that both Greek and Roman art depicts the human form, but in different ways that reflect the values of the culture.

Don't miss the fascinating *City: A Story of Roman Planning and Construction*, *Rome Antics*, and the *Roman City* DVD by David Macaulay. You will most likely find them at your library.

Read the overview of Roman Art and Architecture in this Khan Academy presentation.

https://www.khanacademy.org/humanities/ancient-art-civilizations/roman/x7e914f5b:beginner-guides-to-roman-architecture/a/roman-architecture

You can see art related to the Trojans, including the battle between the Greeks and Trojans at the Louvre in Paris. Just click on images to enlarge them.

https://collections.louvre.fr/en/recherche?q=Troyens&lt=mosaic

Photographer Stevan Kordić presents a beautifully composed exhibition of black and white photographs depicting the art and architecture of ancient Rome. Be aware that this includes a few sculptures of the human form.

https://www.stevan-kordic.info/architecture-in-bw

Historic Context

Eyewitness Ancient Rome by Simon James offers an excellent visual overview of Roman culture. It should be available at your local library.

The Eyewitness to History website offers excellent articles and resources on the ancient world. Read at least six of the Rome-related articles.

http://www.eyewitnesstohistory.com/awfrm.htm

The Romans had many myths that helped them make sense of their world and communicate values. When you read this myth of Echo and Narcissus, you'll notice that even though the story is old, it is still a cautionary tale.

https://excellence-in-literature.com/echo-and-narcissus-by-ovid/

Here's a look at the history of Ancient Rome, as well as some of its most amazing inventions:

https://www.history.com/topics/ancient-rome/ancient-rome

https://www.knowtheromans.co.uk

https://www.history.com/news/10-innovations-that-built-ancient-rome

This Day in History: 03/15/0044 BC—The Ides of March:

https://www.history.com/this-day-in-history/the-ides-of-march

This Roman Army Military Reenactment unit's website offers more information and close-up photos of Roman weapons:

http://www.legionxxiv.org/Default.htm

Here's a brief, literature-focused timeline of Roman literature. Be sure to notice how much was written before *The Aeneid*. We have studied two of the other titles on the list; how many others do you recognize?

https://www.ancient-literature.com/timeline.html

Just for Fun

Feeling confident? Here is a crossword puzzle with clues from *The Aeneid*. It loads very slowly, so you'll have to be patient.

For an additional challenge, here is a crossword puzzle on *Aeneid* characters.

http://games.bestlatin.net/cwblog/2006/10/aeneid-characters-1.html

Assignment Schedule

Week 1

Read *In Search of a Homeland* by Penelope Lively and the author resources on Virgil. Start reading your chosen translation of *The Aeneid*, as well as the context readings. Follow the model in the Formats and Models chapter to write an Author Profile on Virgil. Be sure to refer to your writer's handbook if you have questions about grammar, structure, or style.

Week 2

For each book of *The Aeneid*, use the Literature Summary Model in the Formats and Models chapter to write a brief summary of each book.

As an alternate assignment, you may draw a graphic storyline of the major events of each book (styled like a graphic novel or comic book). In addition to the context links provided, you may use other resources such as your encyclopedia, the library, and quality Internet resources to complete this assignment.

Week 3

Begin drafting a 750-word paper on one of the topics below. I recommend that you follow the writing process outlined in the "How to Write an Essay" chapter, consulting the models in the Formats and Models chapter and your writer's handbook as needed.

1- Model: Literary Analysis Essay and MLA Format Model

Prompt: Discuss what brings about pain and suffering in *The Aeneid*, and consider the role played by fate, the gods, and the individual characters and the choices they make. Which of these do the characters hold responsible for their troubles, and what factors actually seem to be responsible?

2- Model: *The Aeneid* and MLA Format Model

Prompt: Rewrite one of the twelve books of *The Aeneid* in prose. Tell the story with colorful details, making sure that your reader will finish the tale with a vivid understanding of the characters and events. Make this as long as necessary in order to tell a good story.

Turn in the draft at the end of the week, so your writing mentor can evaluate it using the Content standards (Ideas/Concepts and Organization) on the rubric.

Week 4

Use the feedback on the rubric, along with the writing mentor's comments to revise your paper. Before turning in the final draft, be sure you have addressed any issues marked on the evaluation rubric, and verify that the thesis is clear and your essay is well-organized. Use your writer's handbook to check grammar or punctuation so that your essay will be free from mechanical errors. Turn in the essay at the end of the week so that the writing mentor can use the evaluation rubric in the "How to Evaluate" chapter to check your wor.

Module 5.4

Inferno by Dante Alighieri (1265–1321)

Lasciate ogne speranza, voi ch'intrate.
Abandon all hope, ye who enter here.

— Canto 3.[30]

Focus Text

Divine Comedy: Inferno by Dante Alighieri

I recommend reading the Anthony Esolen translation from the well-annotated Modern Library Series or the John Ciardi translation from New American Library. You may also want to get Dorothy Sayers' translation (published by Penguin Classics) just for her commentary and notes.

Clive James provides insight into what makes a good translation as he discusses the philosophy and inspiration behind his own translation of Dante's masterpiece. At the link below to the NPR website, you may listen to the full interview and read an excerpt from James's translation.

http://www.npr.org/2013/04/13/177045282/dantes-beauty-rendered-in-english-in-a-divine-comedy

Honors Text

Paradiso and/or *Purgatorio* by Dante Alighieri

You may choose to also read *Confessions* by Augustine, as it is an interesting contrast.

Literary Period
Medieval

Module Focus

We will learn a great deal about the medieval worldview in Dante's works, and explore a poem that is considered by many to be the pinnacle of the medieval poetic tradition.

Introduction

In Dante's epic poems, he writes about three places—hell, purgatory, and heaven—as he imagines them. Through the three books of the story, he takes a vivid and thought-provoking journey through each of these worlds, encountering famous people and human nature in many different guises.

In the optional resource, *Invitation to the Classics*, the authors assert that the "single, unified theme of the entire *Comedy* is love . . . God is love, and every aspect of his creation, especially humanity, is infused with this divine attribute" and that life is an "arduous search to love the right things in the right way" (99).

Something to think about . . .

Dante's imaginative journey in *Inferno* offers deeply insightful glimpses of human nature, his own life story, and the history and people of his time and place in the world. Remember, though—it's a work of fiction rather than history, biography, or theology. As you read, focus on recognizing truth in the various scenarios. How might Dante's story of a life beyond help us live life now?

Be sure to notice . . .

Inferno is fascinating, but it is full of vivid and terrible images. Even if you are not planning to do the Honors option, be sure to read at least one scene from *Paradiso*, so you can see the starkly contrasting word pictures that Dante paints. Notice how the tone of his writing changes as he depicts hell (the "Inferno") in dark, frightening, language, and heaven in light, beautiful words. This is consistent with the classical meaning of "comedy." In a letter to his patron, Cangrande I della Scala, Dante explains that the pilgrimage from Hell to Paradise is an expression of comedy, since the work begins with the pilgrim's moral confusion and ends with the vision of God.

Context Resources

Readings

If you have *Invitation to the Classics*, read the chapter on Dante. It will help you understand the author's worldview and how the work fits into literary history.

Dr. Gino Casagrande, now a professor emeritus at the University of Wisconsin, has put together a comprehensive online guide to Dante's *Inferno*. Click on the link below to read about the structure of the *Inferno* (there is a text summary below the diagram); if you want to explore further, scroll up to the top of the page, and use the left-hand menu to navigate the site and learn more about the *Divine Comedy* and Dante's life. There is also a helpful Index and Glossary that may help you to identify characters and understand Dante's many cultural references.

http://www.gicas.net/inferno.html#3

The University of Texas at Austin has created Danteworlds, an excellent illustrated online study guide. Please use your own judgment as to whether to use this. The illustrations make the poem easier to understand but may be disturbing to some.

http://danteworlds.laits.utexas.edu

Complete Danteworlds: A Reader's Guide to the Divine Comedy by Guy P. Raffa contains a complete version of the commentary that is excerpted at Danteworlds.

The Princeton Dante Project extensively covers Dante's life and works in an attractive and easy-to-navigate form.

https://dante.princeton.edu/pdp/

World of Dante is another very good resource, sponsored by the University of Virginia. The first link is to the site; the second is to a video orientation movie.

http://www.worldofdante.org

http://www.worldofdante.org/media/Dante_Instructions_640x480.mov

Although Dante's *Divine Comedy: Inferno* is universally recognized as a classic work of literature, various writers have analyzed the relationship between the *Comedy* and the Bible. For two differing viewpoints, see the links below: first a short discussion from a Protestant perspective, then an article on Dante's life and masterpiece from *The Catholic Encyclopedia*. Scroll to the second half to read the section about the "Divina Commedia" (*Divine Comedy*).

https://www.gotquestions.org/Divine-Comedy-Dantes-Inferno.html

https://www.newadvent.org/cathen/04628a.htm

The Living in Hell: Sacred Signs/Secular Meanings in Dante's Inferno is the outline of a 2002 lecture given by Dr. Fajardo-Acosta at Creighton University.

http://fajardo-acosta.com/worldlit/dante/lecture.htm

This introduction, from West Chester University English professor Stacy Esch, may help you put Dante's work into its literary context:

https://excellence-in-literature.com/approaching-the-divine-comedy-by-stacy-esch/

The Author's Life

Dante: Poet, Author, and Proud Florentine by John C. Davenport is a middle-grade biography, and an excellent introduction to Dante as a person. It is available on Amazon.com, or you may find it through your library.

James E. Kiefer has written a number of short biographies of important people in Christian church history, including a thoughtful biography of Dante.

http://elvis.rowan.edu/~kilroy/JEK/09/15.html

You may also read a 1911 biography of Dante at the link below.

https://excellence-in-literature.com/dante-biography/

Poetry

Poetry was obviously very important to Dante. In addition to the works of Virgil, he is known to have enjoyed the work of Brunetto Latini, whose work is discussed on this interesting site:

http://www.florin.ms/Bankers.html

You may be interested to see the difference in style between German lyric poet Walther von der Vogelweide (you will find his biography in your encyclopedia) and Dante. Read at least two poems on each page.

Walther: http://www.dunphy.de/Medieval/Walther

Dante: https://www.planck.com/rhymedtranslations/versetrans.htm

Audio

Your library may have *Inferno* on CD, but you can also download it free at Librivox (this is an amateur production, so check your library first). If you enjoy the poem, you may want to purchase an audio version from www.Audible.com.

https://librivox.org/the-divine-comedy-version-2-dramatic-reading-by-dante-alighieri/

Music

Start with this "Introduction to Medieval Music"—it traces the history of the music Dante most likely heard during his lifetime, covering 13th–14th century music from plainchant through polyphany.

https://excellence-in-literature.com/medieval-music-cynthia-cyrus/

There is a lot of chanting and singing in *Paradiso* and *Purgatorio*, but no singing at all in the *Inferno* (quite understandable). *On Identifying and Performing the Chants in Dante's Divine Comedy* offers interesting insights into the different types and purposes of the chants.

http://www.worldofdante.org/comedy/dante/musicEssay

Thirteenth-Century Polyphony: A Quick Guide to Combinations and Cadences offers a rather scholarly overview of the type of music Dante may have heard during his lifetime.

http://www.medieval.org/emfaq/harmony/13c.html

Video

Watch a brief video of Roberto Benigni reciting the fifth canto in Italian. It will allow you to appreciate the beauty and rhythm in the language of the poem.

https://excellence-in-literature.com/recitation-of-dantes-inferno-by-roberto-benigni/

You might also enjoy this 1911 silent movie of *Inferno*.

https://excellence-in-literature.com/dantes-inferno-the-1911-silent-movie/

Visual Arts

These maps will help you visualize Dante's world:

http://www.worldofdante.org/maps_main.html

Auguste Rodin's sculptural group "The Gates of Hell" is largely inspired by people and events in *Inferno*. Dante is represented by the figure near the top of the gate.

http://www.musee-rodin.fr/en/collections/sculptures/gates-hell

Salvador Dali was commissioned to celebrate Dante's 700th birthday by creating a series of illustrations for *The Divine Comedy*.

https://www.ratbags.com/rsoles/artworks/dali/divinecomedy.htm

Other artists, including William Blake, a writer and artist of the Romantic era, have interpreted Dante's works in various ways. You may view several different artistic interpretations in the World of Dante Gallery. Don't miss Gustave Doré's incredible illustrations.

http://www.worldofdante.org/gallery_main.html

Oxford's Bodlein Library has posted several pages from a dramatically illustrated medieval manuscript of *Divine Comedy*.

https://digital.bodleian.ox.ac.uk/objects/cb1df5f1-7435-468b-8860-d56db988b929/

Historical Context

The "History of Florence" site offers an overview of Florentine history. Note particularly the section about the Guelphs and Ghibellines.

http://www.aboutflorence.com/history-of-Florence.html

Timelines: These detailed timelines provide six different gateways for exploring the history of Dante's birthplace, Florence. The Artists and Writers timeline is especially interesting.

http://timelineflorence.com

More about the Guelphs and Ghibellines:

http://www.dantemass.org/html/guelphs-and-ghibellines.html

Dante Today from Bowdoin College offers a selection of "Citings and Sightings of Dante's Works in Contemporary Culture." Many scholars insist that Dante's work, like Shakespeare's, is as fresh and contemporary as the day he wrote it. The sheer number of citations at this site seems to confirm their belief.

https://research.bowdoin.edu/dante-today/

The great classics of Western Civilization have touched the lives of many generations, and their ideas continue to permeate our culture. Read about the development and history of Western Literature (the literature of Western Civilization, not books about the American West).

https://academic-eb-com.eres.qnl.qa/levels/collegiate/article/Western-literature/108641

Assignment Schedule

Week 1

Read and explore context materials, and begin reading focus text.

Follow the model in the Formats and Models chapter to write an Author Profile. Be sure to refer to your writer's handbook if you have questions about grammar, structure, or style.

Week 2

Read through *Inferno*, considering the questions below. As you read, you may come across words or references that are unfamiliar. Write them down, along with the stanza number, so you can look them up later. As you read through the poem, write a brief summary of each canto. Number each summary with the canto number, so you can use your summary to find examples you wish to quote in your essay. You may also wish to sketch a diagram that will help you visualize the circles of hell.

- In the first canto, how does Dante make the reader aware that this journey is more than just a walk in the woods?
- Why does Dante admire Virgil? Why is or is not he an appropriate guide for Dante?
- How can Dante's journey be compared with the journey of Aeneas?

Week 3

Begin drafting a 750-word paper on the topic below. I recommend that you follow the writing process outlined in the "How to Write an Essay" chapter, consulting the models in the Formats and Models chapter and your writer's handbook as needed.

1- Model: Literary Analysis Essay and MLA Format Model

Prompt: Consider Dante's journey as a necessary path of discovery in order to attain spiritual insight and balance. Discuss what he learns about himself and about sin, and how he is changed by the experience..

2- Model: Literary Analysis Essay and MLA Format Model

Prompt: Dante's vision of hell has a carefully structured hierarchy, which ranks sins according to their seriousness and prescribes penalties for each. Discuss this structure of punishments, considering what it reveals about Dante's vision of the individual, society, and the various ways these can become corrupt.

Turn in the draft at the end of the week, so your writing mentor can evaluate it using the Content standards (Ideas/Concepts and Organization) on the rubric.

Week 4

Use the feedback on the rubric along with the writing mentor's comments to revise your paper. Before turning in the final draft, be sure you have addressed any issues marked on the evaluation rubric and verify that the thesis is clear and your essay is well-organized. Use your writer's handbook to check grammar or punctuation so that your essay will be free from mechanical errors. Turn in the essay at the end of the week so that the writing mentor can use the evaluation rubric in the "How to Evaluate" chapter to check your work

Module 5.5

Don Quixote by Miguel de Cervantes (1547–1616)
Tell me thy company and I will tell thee what thou art.

—*Don Quixote* (vol. III, pt. II, ch. XXIII)

Focus Text

Don Quixote by Miguel de Cervantes (1547–1616)

I recommend the Tobias Smollet translation, published by Modern Library, with an excellent introduction by Carlos Fuentes. This edition also contains a brief biography of Cervantes and other helpful notes, including detailed explanatory end notes.

Honors Text

The Pickwick Papers by Charles Dickens (This is another novel in the picaresque tradition.)

Literary Period

Spanish Golden Age/Renaissance

Module Focus

As you read this long, often funny story, you will consider what Cervantes is showing about truth, justice, and reality, and learn about the conventions of the picaresque novel.

Introduction

Don Quixote has been called the greatest novel in history, the first modern novel, one of the funniest novels of all time, and it is found on most "top 100" lists. According to the authors of *Invitation to the Classics*, it "provides a context for serious reflection on the meaning of human existence" and "bears witness to the clash between Christian ideals and the conflicting images of reality in a rapidly changing world." This is why the story has remained alive and relevant for over 400 years.

In the story, our protagonist, Don Quixote de la Mancha, is influenced by his reading of chivalrous romances. He believes that he must become a hero, and along with his faithful companion, Sancho Panza, he puts together a homemade suit of armor and sets off on a series of adventures. The story has both comic and tragic elements and is said to have inspired many other works of literature by writers such as Charles Dickens, Graham Greene, and humorist P. G. Wodehouse.

Something to think about . . .

Miguel de Cervantes lived and worked during the same period in history—the Renaissance, Reformation, and Counter-Reformation—as William Shakespeare, John Calvin, and Edmund Spenser. It was a time of astonishing creativity and exploration, as well as fierce debates about faith and life. As you read through this module, think about why this was such an eventful era, and how its color and drama are shown in the art, literature, and music of the day.

Be sure to notice . . .

Reading books was of paramount importance to characters of various social classes in *Don Quixote*, including Quixote himself, Cardenio, Marcella, the New Arcadians, the curate, the innkeeper, and the barber. Notice also that *Don Quixote* was published fewer than 175 years after Johannes Gutenberg brought mechanical moveable type printing to Europe. How might these two facts be related? How is Gutenberg's invention significant for ordinary people?

Context Resources

Readings

If you have *Invitation to the Classics,* read the discussion of *Don Quixote* and the section on Spanish Classics.

Look up the definition of "quixotic" in your dictionary and write it down. Also review the definition of "picaresque novel."

Why read Don Quixote? This delightful article by Dr. Brian T. Kelley of Thomas Aquinas College offers a number of reasons.

https://www.thomasaquinas.edu/news/don-quixote-and-glory-life-come-why-we-study-cervantes

Creighton University professor, Dr. Fidel Fajardo-Acosta, has posted some thought-provoking questions about *Don Quixote*. You may wish to print the study questions and refer to them as you read.

http://fajardo-acosta.com/worldlit/cervantes/quixote.htm#study_questions

Learn about Cervantes' legacy and influence through this brief article on the USC website. Scroll down to read "The Legacy of Cervantes."

https://libguides.usc.edu/don_quixote

Cervantes was heavily influenced by the works of Christian Humanist philosopher Desiderius Erasmus, especially *In Praise of Folly*. Erasmus created one of the first parallel translations of the Bible, with Greek and Latin text side-by-side in columns. This translation was reportedly among those used by Martin Luther for his German translation. Read about Erasmus in your encyclopedia, and think about how his worldview compares or contrasts with a biblical worldview.

https://www.erasmus.org/index.cfm?itm_name=erasmus-EN

It is helpful to see a timeline of events during Cervantes' life. This one is not a scholarly resource, but was put together by a group of people who spent the summer of 2007 reading *Don Quixote* as a group project. The essay on "Don Quixote and the Invention of the Modern Novel," also on this blog, is very interesting as well.

https://tiltingatwindmillsblog.wordpress.com/2007/04/30/historical-timeline-spain-1510-1616/

The Author's Life

Miguel De Cervantes by Barbara Keevil Parker and Duane F. Parker is a decent short biography. Check your library, or find it used on Amazon.com. If you cannot find it, you may rely on the biography in the recommended edition of *Don*

Quixote, or read any good, brief biography of Cervantes from your library, in an encyclopedia, or at one or more of the sites below.

https://www.biography.com/writer/miguel-de-cervantes

https://excellence-in-literature.com/miguel-de-cervantes-biography/

Poetry

Author G. K. Chesterton wrote a poem about the battle in which Miguel de Cervantes is said to have been seriously wounded. Read "Lepanto," and listen to the two-part reading of it at the YouTube videos below. They are "talking head" videos, so you do not need to watch—just listen to the rhythm and cadence of Chesterton's language (you will notice his love of alliteration), and visualize the scenes unfolding.

https://excellence-in-literature.com/lepanto-by-g-k-chesterton

You can read more about the Battle of Lepanto and its significance here:

https://www.newworldencyclopedia.org/entry/Battle_of_Lepanto

There were many excellent poets during the Spanish Golden Age, including Francisco de Quevedo and Luis de Góngora. Here is a poem from each of them, plus one additional poem by de Góngora about de Quevedo, all translated by Alix Ingber, Professor Emerita of Spanish at Sweet Briar College.

"Presenting the brevity of life now and how inconsequential one's past life seems."

http://ingber.spanish.sbc.edu/cgi-bin/sonnets.py?activity=get_poem&poem_id=quevedo11

"Concerning an ailing wayfarer who fell in love where he was lodged."

http://ingber.spanish.sbc.edu/cgi-bin/sonnets.py?activity=get_poem&poem_id=gongora12

"To Don Francisco de Quevedo" (attributed to Góngora)

http://ingber.spanish.sbc.edu/cgi-bin/sonnets.py?activity=get_poem&poem_id=gongora03

Audio

Don Quixote is a very long novel, so you may want to break it up by listening to portions of it. You may get a good professional recording from your library or

Audible.com, or listen to a free amateur audio version from LibriVox (the professional version is much, much better).

http://librivox.org/don-quixote-vol-1-by-miguel-de-cervantes-saavedra/

http://librivox.org/don-quixote-vol-2-by-miguel-de-cervantes-saavedra/

Music

Tomás Luis de Victoria, a 16th-century Spanish classical composer, is known for his beautiful polyphonic choral works in the tradition of Palestrina. Classic Cat links to free online sources for hearing some of his beautiful music. You have to click several links to arrive at the recording, but it is worth it if you enjoy choral music. The second link will take you to a Spanish-language site with many Victoria recordings. Listen to as many as you like—they are peaceful and beautiful (and many of them are fun to sing).

https://classiccat.net/victoria_tl_de/index.php

https://www.uma.es/victoria/mp3.html

Have you ever heard the song "The Impossible Dream"? It's from *Man Of La Mancha*, a 1972 musical that is loosely based on *Don Quixote*. Even though it doesn't hew exactly to the book, there's enough of the story to make it worth watching.

Video

I have not seen any of the many *Don Quixote* movies available, but I have heard that the 2000 Hallmark version with John Lithgow in the title role is a good choice. You may want to consult a movie guide for more information.

http://www.imdb.com/title/tt0181212/

A short clip from the 2000 version is available here:

https://excellence-in-literature.com/don-quixote-2000-film-clip/

Lope de Vega is the most famous playwright of Spain's Golden Age, and his colorful dramas have been compared to Shakespeare's, and some are still performed.

Visual Arts

El Greco (Doménikos Theotokópoulos) is one of the most famous artists who lived and worked in Spain during Cervantes' lifetime. Read about his life and unique style at the National Gallery of Art. Notice especially his famous landscape, the *View of Toledo* at the first link below.

https://excellence-in-literature.com/renaissance-art/

As you read about El Greco and view more of his paintings at the National Gallery of Art site, consider whether the mood of his paintings feels similar to the mood of Don Quixote.

https://www.nga.gov/collection/artist-info.1356.html#works

Another painter of Cervantes' time was Diego Velázquez, court artist for King Phillip II. He painted portraits and historical scenes in a realistic style comparable to that of Dutch masters such as Johannes Vermeer and Frans Hals. Read more about these painters in an art history encyclopedia or online, and reflect on what they illustrate about the historical period.

https://www.diegovelazquez.org

The 1781 edition of *Don Quixote* contained fifteen detailed illustrations that reflect the mood of the story.

http://cervantes.dh.tamu.edu/veri/Bowle/index.htm

Historical Context

It is important to understand the Protestant Reformation and the Counter-Reformation as a historical context for Cervantes' writing. Read about them in your encyclopedia or at the references below. If you enjoy history, the History Guide site is well worth exploring. It is an outstanding site full of interesting articles, all written by a homeschool-friendly college professor, Dr. Steven Kreis.

The Medieval Synthesis and the Renaissance Discovery of Man

https://excellence-in-literature.com/
the-medieval-synthesis-and-the-discovery-of-man-by-steven-kreis/

The Medieval Synthesis Under Attack: Savonarola and the Protestant Reformation

https://excellence-in-literature.com/
the-medieval-synthesis-under-attack-by-steven-kreis/

The Renaissance was another important influence on Cervantes' work. Read about it in your encyclopedia or at the resources below:

Eyewitness *Renaissance* by Alison Cole (library or https://amzn.to/3vwviSr)

https://excellence-in-literature.com/history-of-the-renaissance-by-bamber-gascoigne/

Assignment Schedule

Week 1

Read and explore context materials, and begin watching, listening to, and/or reading *Don Quixote*.

Follow the model in the Formats and Models chapter to write an Author Profile. Be sure to refer to your writer's handbook if you have questions about grammar, structure, or style.

Week 2

Continue studying the focus work and context resources. As you listen to or read *Don Quixote*, note that it is divided into two volumes, with four "books" in each volume. Write an interesting summary (up to 300 words per book) of each of the eight books, noting the principle events and characters. Select a quotation from the book or from another source, to use as an epigraph for each of your summaries.

Alternatively, you may sketch a summary of each book, making sure that the sketches convey the main ideas of the story. As above, choose a quote to use as a caption or epigraph for each sketch.

Week 3

Begin drafting a 750-word paper on one of the topics below. I recommend that you follow the writing process outlined in the "How to Write an Essay" chapter, consulting the models in the Formats and Models chapter and your writer's handbook as needed.

1- Model: Literary Analysis Essay and MLA Format Model

Prompt: Consider the ways in which truth and justice are depicted in *Don Quixote*, paying particular attention to the historical and social context of the work (the Protestant Reformation, the Counter-Reformation, and the Renaissance). Use brief textual quotes to support your thesis.

2- Model: Literary Analysis Essay and MLA Format Model

Prompt: Reading books was of paramount importance to many characters, including Don Quixote, Cardenio, Marcella, the New Arcadians, the curate, the innkeeper, and the barber. Why do you think this might have been? Write an essay in which you consider the role of reading in the lives of these characters. Be sure to discuss your impression of what Cervantes is trying communicate about reading and books. Support your argument with brief, appropriate quotes from the text.

3- Model: Compare/Contrast Essay and MLA Format Model

Prompt: Compare and contrast the events, people, and places in the three expeditions or "sallies" of Don Quixote. Why do you think there were three sallies, rather than one long journey? How do the events of each of the sallies contribute to the development of the characters of Don Quixote and Sancho Panza? Use brief textual quotes to support your thesis.

4-Model: *Don Quixote* and the Journalism Story Structure article

Prompt: Write two newspaper articles, each retelling a scene from *Don Quixote* as if you were a journalist observing the events. Suggested scene choices include the windmill scene, the captives tale, or the story of Quixote's love for Dulcinea, but you may choose other scenes if you prefer. Make the articles as long as necessary in order to tell a good story, with the two articles together equaling 750 words or more.

https://excellence-in-literature.com/journalism-story-structure-by-mark-grabowski/

Turn in the draft at the end of the week, so your writing mentor can evaluate it using the Content standards (Ideas/Concepts and Organization) on the rubric.

Week 4

Use the feedback on the rubric along with the writing mentor's comments to revise your paper. Before turning in the final draft, be sure you have addressed any issues marked on the evaluation rubric, and verify that the thesis is clear and your essay is well-organized. Use your writer's handbook to check grammar or punctuation so that your essay will be free from mechanical errors. Turn in the essay at the end of the week so that the writing mentor can use the evaluation rubric in the "How to Evaluate" chapter to check your work

Module 5.6

Les Misérables by Victor Hugo (1802–1885)

*"Have courage for the great sorrows of life and patience for the small ones;
and when you have laboriously accomplished your daily task, go to sleep in peace.
God is awake."*

—Victor Hugo

Focus Text

Les Misérables by Victor Hugo (1802–1885)

The Charles E. Wilbour translation was created shortly after Hugo wrote the book, so it captures some of the flavor of Hugo's era. An alternative that might be easier for a modern reader is the Norman Denny translation from Penguin Classics or the Julie Rose translation by Modern Library. You may go to Amazon and click on the "Look Inside" image to read a page of each and determine which translation you prefer.

Honors Texts

The Hunchback of Notre-Dame by Victor Hugo OR

Democracy in America by Alexis de Tocqueville (You may select the abridged version.)

Literary Period

Romantic

Module Focus

You will become familiar with nineteenth-century France, observe the transition from the Romantic to the Realist style, and learn about Victor Hugo, a beloved and enduring French novelist, playwright, and poet.

Introduction

Les Misérables ranks among my top ten favorite books of all time. I am delighted to share it with you, and I hope you will read it several times during your life, as each time you will find more to enjoy. This absorbing tale of love and justice focuses on the life of Jean Valjean (pronounced Zhahn Val-zhahn), who has just spent nineteen years in prison for stealing a loaf of bread. As we follow Valjean and Javert, the relentless detective who dogs his steps for many years, Hugo paints a compelling picture of the nature of justice and injustice, and the overwhelming redemptive power of love.

Something to think about . . .

Hugo is reported to be an exceptionally disciplined writer, producing twenty or more pages of prose or over one hundred lines of poetry every day. This is a good example for anyone who wants to become a writer. Don't wait for the perfect inspiration, the ideal weather, absolute silence, a new red notebook, or a better purple pen. Just make it a priority to sit down and write, every single day. If you are faithful at doing this and you seek constructive feedback from masters in the craft of writing, you can become a writer.

Be sure to notice . . .

Jean Valjean's experiences reflect Victor Hugo's values and his empathy with victims of injustice. As you read through *Les Misérables*, notice scenes in which Hugo illustrates the difference between justice and mercy. Does the emotion and reality of these scenes make abstract concepts easier to understand? What does Hugo show us about justice and mercy, and how does it compare with the depiction of these ideas in ancient works such as *Antigone* or the biblical text of James 2:12-13?

Context Resources

Readings

Invitation to the Classics ed. by Cowan and Guinness: If you own or can borrow this book, read the section on French Classics (253–258). The editors approach their topic from a worldview that leads to a slightly different angle of analysis from Norton's.

Norton Anthology of World Literature Vol. E (if you have it): Hugo biography and poem, and other works of the time. Just browse a bit to see what was happening in the literary, spiritual, and political arenas.

The Penguin Reading Guide offers a thoughtful introduction and a few study questions for *Les Misérables* and Victor Hugo.

https://www.penguin.com/static/html/classics/readingguides/lesmiserables.php

This insightful article by Dr. Michael Morales explores the tension between law, grace, and redemption in *Les Misérables*.

https://www.ligonier.org/learn/articles/law-grace-redemption-les-miserables/

Here is a free downloadable study by Theatre Under the Stars based on the *Les Misérables* musical. It has background information on France, the social and political unrest of the time, the cultural conditions seen in *Les Misérables*, and details about the creation of the musical. I suggest reading all the way through it during the first week.

https://web.archive.org/web/20150404051244/www.tuts.com/Images/SeasonShow-Docs/LesMiserables_StudyGuide.pdf

Optional: This French-language site offers information on *Les Misérables*. If you are studying French, you may want to practice the language by reading some of the context information here.

http://www.alalettre.com/victor-hugo-oeuvres-miserables.php

The Author's Life

Read at least one short biography of Victor Hugo from the library or at the link below. Try to gain a good understanding of his life and works before you begin the novel.

https://excellence-in-literature.com/victor-hugo-biography/

Victor Hugo wrote an eloquent appeal to America on behalf the abolitionist John Brown. This is a remarkable example of persuasive writing—does it make you feel more or less inclined to agree with Hugo's position?

https://excellence-in-literature.com/victor-hugo-a-persuasive-letter-regarding-john-brown/

In 1836, Swedish professor and lecturer Carl August Hagberg met Victor Hugo. Enjoy his interesting, brief description of Hugo and his home.

http://archive.is/xw5Ch

Poetry

The Academy of American Poets offers "A Brief Guide to Romanticism."

https://poets.org/text/brief-guide-romanticism

Many European Romantic writers wrote both poetry and prose, and Victor Hugo is no exception. As you read *Les Misérables* and Hugo's poems, observe the conventions of Romanticism in both prose and poetry. Here are a few translated samples of his poetry.

http://www.gavroche.org/vhugo/vhpoetry/

http://gbarto.com/hugo/index.html —Read at least three poems linked from the Poetry column.

"Demain dès l'aube" was written in remembrance of Hugo's daughter. Listen to this poem being read aloud:

https://excellence-in-literature.com/victor-hugo-poem-read-aloud/

"Boaz Asleep" is a Romantic-style retelling of the story of Boaz and Ruth.

https://excellence-in-literature.com/boaz-asleep-by-victor-hugo/

Alphonse de Lamartine was another French writer, poet, and politician of Hugo's era. "The Lake," one of his most famous poems, has been translated at the Consolation website.

https://www.consolatio.com/2007/12/lamartine-man-h.html

Marceline Desbordes-Valmore was a French Romantic poet whose work touched on home, family, and faith, among other topics. You may read a few of her poems and her life story at the Women's Poet Timeline Project.

https://www.mezzocammin.com/timeline/timeline.php?vol=timeline&iss=1700&cat=80&page=valmore

English poet Alfred, Lord Tennyson was a fan of Victor Hugo and wrote the short poem below as a tribute.

https://www.bartleby.com/360/7/24.html

Audio

I recommend the unabridged audio version of *Les Misérables* translated by Charles E. Wilbour and narrated by the outstanding narrator Frederick Davidson. This version is well worth hearing. At the very least, you will know that all the French names and places are correctly pronounced.

https://amzn.to/33O55CL

A free amateur audio version of *Les Misérables* is available from Librivox in five volumes. Since this is not a professional recording, keep in mind that pronunciation may not be standard. Here is the link for volume one; search for "Les Misérables" in the Catalog to find the other volumes.

https://librivox.org/group/296

Here's a guide to help you correctly pronounce names as you are reading. This chart offers written and recorded pronunciations for each of the characters.

http://www.tdej.org/2010_character_breakdown_vocal_range.php

Music

Composer Camille Saint-Saens was a friend and admirer of Victor Hugo, and composed the "Hymne à Victor Hugo" which you can hear at the first link below. After Hugo's death, he wrote the tribute that you will find at the second link.

https://excellence-in-literature.com/victor-hugo-resources/

http://classicalmusicguide.com/viewtopic.php?t=16924

Victor Hugo in Music: Mélodies on the poems of Victor Hugo is a CD of compositions set to Hugo's poetry. You can read more about it and listen to samples at Presto Classical. If you enjoy it, you may be able to borrow it from your library.

https://www.prestomusic.com/classical/products/7977719--victor-hugo-in-music

Music scholar M. Tevfik Dorak has posted an interesting article on the music of the Romantic era with a detailed description of its development and ideas.

http://dorakmt.tripod.com/music/romantic.html

This site offers a synopsis of the musical *Les Misérables* with clips from each song. It's better to watch the entire musical if you can, but the brief excerpts here are an introduction if you're not able to watch the whole thing.

http://www.mtishows.com/show_detail.asp?showid=000134

Listen to the French national anthem, "La Marseillaise," at the link below.

https://excellence-in-literature.com/la-marseillaise-sung-by-placido-domingo/

Here is a band version of "La Marseillaise," with an English translation of the words.

https://excellence-in-literature.com/band-version-of-la-marseillaise-with-lyrics/

Video

If you can attend a live performance of the *Les Misérables* musical, do so. Although considerably shortened due to time constraints, it is faithful to Hugo's novel and is a beautiful and moving drama. If you cannot see it live, watch the video (get it from the library or from an online streaming service).

The 2012 film of *Les Misérables* starring Hugh Jackman is rated PG-13 and contains mature themes. Please make your own family decision about whether or not you would feel comfortable watching this; the links below provide more information on what you can expect to encounter in this film.

At IMDB, see Parents Guide in the "Storyline" section:

https://www.imdb.com/title/tt1707386/

Decent Films 60-Second Review:

http://www.decentfilms.com/blog/lesmiserables-60sec

Visual Arts

Look at the art of the French Romantic period in *The Annotated Mona Lisa* or other art history book, and read about it at the link below:

https://about-france.com/art/neoclassicism-romanticism.htm

Using an art history encyclopedia, look up the following French artists of the nineteenth century: Jean-Baptiste-Camille Corot, Rosa Bonheur, Eugène Delacroix, Jean-François Millet, and Gustave Courbet. Notice ways in which their styles are similar or different from one another. There are many more wonderful artists of the Romantic era, so feel free to explore further in your art history book.

One painting that seems to capture the mood of the age is *Napoleon Crossing the Alps* by Jacques-Louis David. See what you think!

https://excellence-in-literature.com/wp-content/uploads/2013/08/JLDavid_Napol_Mal.jpg

The French Romantics: Literature and the Visual Arts 1800-1840 by David Wakefield– If your local library or nearby college has this book, the chapter on Victor Hugo is worth reading for its interesting analysis of the connection between literature and the arts during this historic period.

Norton Anthology of World Literature Vol. E: If you have this book, look at the art in the center of the book, noting particularly the French art. Consider what these paintings communicate about the worldview of the artist. If you do not have this volume of the anthology, you may look at an art history book or website for examples of the art of this period. I believe the visual arts offer insight into the ideas that shaped the literature of the time.

Historical Context

The June Rebellion, also known as the Paris Uprising of 1832, had an impact on Victor Hugo's life and thoughts, and is included toward the end of *Les Misérables*. Many people confuse this Rebellion with the French Revolution, but this article by Cynthia Haven will help you understand this event and its place in the story.

https://bookhaven.stanford.edu/2012/12/
enjoy-les-miserables-but-please-get-your-history-straight-first/

The French Revolution happened before Hugo was born, but its events continued to be influential well into his lifetime. Browse through this interesting site created by George Mason University.

https://revolution.chnm.org

Here are two good overviews of Romanticism, written by college professors. It is always a good idea to read more than one source for any idea. Different scholars or authors focus on different aspects of a topic, so reading from more than one source tends to create a more balanced body of knowledge. It also gives you more information to draw upon as you write your papers.

https://excellence-in-literature.com/introduction-to-romanticism-from-lilia-melani/

https://brians.wsu.edu/2016/10/12/romanticism/

Read about Napoleon, Romanticism, and the Enlightenment in your encyclopedia or at the History Guide website listed below. "Europe and the Superior Being: Napoleon" and "The Romantic Critique of the Enlightenment" are two excellent articles that provide intellectual context for Hugo's writing.

https://excellence-in-literature.com/napoleon/

https://excellence-in-literature.com/the-romantic-era-by-steven-kreis/

Norton Anthology of World Literature Vol. E: If you have this, read the Introduction to "Revolution and Romanticism in Europe and America" with map and timeline, which is a fascinating look at a remarkable period of history. Observe the connections between literature, art, religion, and politics, and note who was living and writing during Hugo's lifetime.

Places to Go

The city of Paris plays an important part in *Les Misérables*, and this Mt. Holyoke site on Victor Hugo's Paris offers an excellent virtual tour.

https://www.mtholyoke.edu/courses/rschwart/hist255-s01/mapping-paris/Mapping_Home.html

Victor Hugo lived at Hauteville House, on the island of Guernsey in the English Channel, for more than 10 years while in exile from France. His French apartment and this house have been preserved and are open for visits, but you can see quite a few photos at the two pages below. Click the EN at the top of the page for an English translation of the text.

https://www.maisonsvictorhugo.paris.fr/en/museum-collections/house-visit-guernsey

https://www.maisonsvictorhugo.paris.fr/en/museum-collections/place-des-vosges-apartment-visit

Just for Fun

Gavroche, one of the primary characters in *Les Misérables*, is reportedly named after Victor Hugo's cat.

As you browse through information about historical and literary figures, you will come across a few myths. Here is a brief article on the persistent rumor that *Les Misérables* holds a record for the longest sentence in literature.

http://gavroche.org/vhugo/sentence.shtml

Assignment Schedule

Week 1

Begin reading the context resources and the novel, and follow the model in the Formats and Models chapter to write an Author Profile. Be sure to refer to your writer's handbook if you have questions about grammar, structure, or style.

Week 2

Write an Approach Paper on *Les Misérables*. You will find the format and a sample paper in the Formats and Models chapter. In addition to the context links I have provided, you may use other resources such as your encyclopedia, the library, and quality Internet resources to complete this assignment.

Week 3

Begin drafting a 750-word paper on one of the topics below. I recommend that you follow the writing process outlined in the "How to Write an Essay" chapter, consulting the models in the Formats and Models chapter and your writer's handbook as needed.

1- Model: Literary Analysis Essay and MLA Format Model

Prompt: In the preface to *Les Misérables*, Hugo wrote,

> As long as there shall exist, by virtue of law and custom, a social damnation artificially creating hells in the midst of civilization . . . ; while the three great problems of this century, the degradation of man in the proletariat, the subjection of women through hunger, the atrophy of the child by darkness, continue unresolved; . . . while ignorance and poverty persist on earth, books like this cannot fail to be of value.

Write an essay in which you consider how this statement aligns with the ideals of the French Revolution. Discuss how Hugo used various characters such as Jean Valjean, Fantine, Eponine and Gavroche Thénardier, Champmathieu, or others to portray the conditions he describes in the preface, and consider how his portrayal of each character's difficulties not only describes the problem, but suggests a solution. Be sure to provide specific textual support for your thesis.

2- Model: *Les Misérables* and MLA Format Model

Prompt: Write at least five letters from Inspector Javert to his immediate supervisor, reporting on the progress of his pursuit of Jean Valjean. Write at least one letter for each of the five book sections, and be sure to summarize Javert's efforts in his own voice, which will change as the story goes on. Decide whether he would sound self-righteous, defensive, triumphant, defeated, or some other emotion, and make the letters reflect that. This should take at least 1000 words, and should be a long as necessary to sound authentic (as you can tell from the novel, writers in the 19th century were very wordy and usually formal).

Week 4

Use the feedback on the rubric along with the writing mentor's comments to revise your paper. Before turning in the final draft, be sure you have addressed any issues marked on the evaluation rubric, and verify that the thesis is clear and your essay is well-organized. Use your writer's handbook to check grammar or punctuation so that your essay will be free from mechanical errors. Turn in the essay at the end of the week so that the writing mentor can use the evaluation rubric in the "How to Evaluate" chapter to check your work

Module 5.7

Russian Literature Selections

Man, so long as he remains free, has no more constant and agonizing anxiety than to find as quickly as possible someone to worship.

—Fyodor Dostoyevsky

Focus Text

You will read selections from *The Portable Nineteenth Century Russian Reader* edited by George Gibian. Read the Introduction of the book; then for each selection listed below, begin by reading the author profile at the beginning of the chapter. Finally, read the selections assigned below.

- Aleksandr Pushkin- "The Bronze Horseman"
- Nikolay Gogol- "Easter Sunday;" "In Praise of Russian Peasants;" "On the Character of the Russians;" "The Controversy over Gogol's Selected Passages"
- Ivan Turgenev- "On the Russian Language" and "Bezhin Meadow" (The latter story is linked here: https://excellence-in-literature.com/bezhin-meadow-by-ivan-turgenev/.)
- Fyodor Dostoyevsky- "The Grand Inquisitor" (from *The Brothers Karamazov*)
- Leo Tolstoy- "The Death of Ivan Ilych" and "How Literature Teaches Us about Moral and Psychological Life"
- Anton Chekhov- "Uncle Vanya"

- Russian Folk Proverbs
- "Three Questions" by Leo Tolstoy

https://excellence-in-literature.com/three-questions-by-leo-tolstoy/

Honors Texts

The Brothers Karamazov OR *Crime and Punishment* by Fyodor Dostoyevsky OR *The Gulag Archipelago* by Aleksandr Solzhenitsyn OR the remainder of the *Russian Reader*.

NOTE: These books are challenging in their themes and content—the Russians simply don't seem to write about happy things. You may want to consult your parents about which, if any, of these options is appropriate for you.

Literary Period

Realist

Module Focus

You will observe the change from Romanticism to Realism in literature and art, and will develop an understanding of the 19th-century Russian worldview and literary style.

Introduction

The literature of an era or a nation usually reflects the political and social conditions of that time and place. Life in Russia has never been easy, and Russian literature reflects that. As you read through the assigned texts, focus on discovering common themes and trying to understand what created the conditions and worldview that would produce literature like this.

In "Out of the Russian Rage," the Russian literature section of David L. Larson's *In the Company of the Creative: A Christian Reader's Guide to Great Literature and Its Themes*, Larson suggests that "'Mother Russia' seems almost a womb for the world, vast geographically and historically. One thousand years of Russian Orthodoxy so indelibly marked this diverse people that neither czars nor communists could alter it" (461). See what you think as you read through the module.

Something to think about . . .

How do the themes in these readings illuminate the causes of repeated turmoil in Russian history?

Be sure to notice . . .

As you read through these works, think back to the 19th-century American and British writers you have read in previous levels of *Excellence in Literature*. How do the lives, experiences, and themes of the Russian authors compare with their American and British contemporaries? How is this reflected in the art, music, and poetry of each country?

Context Resources

Readings

Begin by reading Washington State University professor Paul Brian's introduction to 19th-Century Russian Literature.

https://brians.wsu.edu/2016/10/12/19th-century-russian-literature/

Study the "Chronology" that begins on page xvii of *The Portable Nineteenth Century Russian Reader*, and consider how the political and social events may have affected writers, artists, and musicians during this century. The timeline below offers additional details that you may find helpful.

http://sites.fas.harvard.edu/~lac50/Timeline/index.cgi

Read the synopsis of the Realist period in literature in the Worldview chapter of this study guide.

Read about "Realism, Naturalism, and Symbolism" in the *Norton Anthology of World Literature, Volume E,* or at the link below. This will help you recognize the ideas and worldview behind the literature, art, and music of this era.

https://literariness.org/2018/01/08/realism-and-naturalism-in-europe-and-america/

These study guides written by college professors may help you to understand "The Grand Inquisitor."

Bruce Foltz, Eckerd College

https://www.academia.edu/20243165/Dostoevsky_Study_and_Reading_Guide

Steven Alan Samson, Liberty University:

https://digitalcommons.liberty.edu/cgi/viewcontent.cgi?referer=&httpsredir=1&article=1190&context=gov_fac_pubs

Optional: In "Ivan Karamazov's Mistake," an essay on the First Things blog, you can read a bit about the philosophical underpinnings of *The Brothers Karamazov*.

https://www.firstthings.com/article/2002/12/ivan-karamazovs-mistake

The Author's Life

Read the brief biographies at the beginning of each chapter in the *Reader* and the resources below.

Pushkin: https://excellence-in-literature.com/pushkin-biography/

Dostoevsky: https://excellence-in-literature.com/dostoevsky-biography/

Dostoevsky Timeline: https://en.rodovid.org/wk/Person:341394

Turgenev: https://excellence-in-literature.com/turgenev-biography/

Tribute: https://excellence-in-literature.com/turgenev-tribute-by-henry-james/

Tolstoy: https://excellence-in-literature.com/leo-tolstoy-biography/

Chekhov: https://excellence-in-literature.com/chekhov-biography/

Poetry

Here are some translations of the poetry of Aleksandr Pushkin. This is not a scholarly site; it was created by a Latvian computer scientist who is a Pushkin fan. The translations are by various people, so not necessarily lyrically perfect. Choose at least three poems, copy them into a text file, and read them thoughtfully. What seem to be Pushkin's themes?

http://www.poetryloverspage.com/poets/pushkin/pushkin_ind.html

Russian Poet Anna Akhmatova was born late in the 19th century and lived a fascinating life full of drama and tragedy. Visit the links below to watch a brief video overview of her life; then read more about her and some of her poetry. The last site is not an academic site, but the translations seem exceptionally well done and worth reading. Akhmatova is a fascinating character, so do not miss her!

https://excellence-in-literature.com/anna-akhmatova-film-trailer/

http://www.uvm.edu/~sgutman/Akhmatova.htm

https://sites.google.com/site/poetryandtranslations/anna-akhmatova

About Pushkin:

https://www.professorcarol.com/2013/09/17/the-poet-pushkin/

Audio

Many of the assigned works can be found as professional audiobooks on Amazon or Audible. You may also find free amateur recordings at Librivox. Just go to the link below and search for the author's last name.

http://librivox.org

The Brothers Karamazov

https://amzn.to/2S7OA1L

Music

If you can attend a live performance of the opera *Eugene Onegin* (also spelled *Evgeny Onegin*), do so. If you cannot see it live, watch it on video. This beautiful opera is based on Aleksandr Sergeyevich Pushkin's famous novel in verse, with a musical score by Pyotr Ilyich Tchaikovsky. Here is an outline of the opera from Metropolitan Opera.

https://www.metopera.org/user-information/synopses-archive/eugene-onegin

Complete recording of *Eugene Onegin*: https://youtu.be/7oTpS_nvnrM

BBC (In Our Time) podcast on *Eugene Onegin* https://youtu.be/Iozr_QKL6iI

https://www.professorcarol.com/2017/03/01/captivated-pushkin/

Note: If you are not familiar with opera, you might want to get Professor Carol Reynolds course, *A Night at the Opera*, to help you understand it. Opera is a beautiful art form of its own. It is not intended to be realistic like a 21st-century movie, nor is it intended to be purely a musical performance. Like modern musicals, it frames beautiful music in a story setting, creating something that can be funny, moving, or simply exquisite. One of the purposes of *Excellence in Literature* is to help you learn about literature in its cultural context, and opera combines the best of music and drama to create an unforgettable experience. I hope you'll take the opportunity to appreciate it!

https://www.professorcarol.com/night-at-the-opera/

You may watch this short video clip of Russian singer Anna Netrebko performing a song from the *Eugene Onegin* opera:

https://excellence-in-literature.com/opera-eugene-onegin-scene-sung-by-netrebko-at-metropolitan-opera/

Listen to the music of Modest Mussorgsky, Nikolai Rimsky-Korsakov, and Alexander Borodin, three of the most prominent Russian composers. They were part of a group known as "The Five," who focused on producing music that was distinctively Russian, rather than European. Your library may have recordings of the work of these composers, or you may visit an online streaming service and enter each composer's name to hear samples of his music.

Read this very interesting article on Tchaikovsky and the Five. Please note that Wikipedia is not a primary source, and I do not use it for any final research. However, it can be useful for a brief introduction to a topic as long as you are able to verify any information gleaned there and provide more reliable sources as a citation.

https://en.wikipedia.org/wiki/Pyotr_Ilyich_Tchaikovsky_and_The_Five

Listen to some of Tchaikovsky's beautiful music at Magazzini Sonori, an Italian site that offers many good clips. The site language is Italian, but you do not need to know the language; just click on the titles of each clip in the right column. A new page will open, and you can click on the "start" arrow to play the piece. If your browser has a translator, just set the language to English and most of the text will immediately be translated. Enjoy!

http://www.magazzini-sonori.it/esplora/compositori/ajkovskij.aspx

This interesting article on Turgenev and Tchaikovsky provides a glimpse into the relationship between these two great Russian creatives.

https://web.archive.org/web/20120329095713/http://www.turgenevmusica.info/en/tchaikovsky.html

Video

Here is a link to brief video clips of Leo Tolstoy at various times in his life and at his death. Note the vast crowds that accompany his coffin in the funeral procession.

https://excellence-in-literature.com/video-of-leo-tolstoy/

Here is a brief history of Russia from 1533 to the present. It is illustrated by birds-eye view maps, so that you can see the size of the country. Remember, YouTube can't be cited as a scholarly source; they are just a starting point for further research.

https://excellence-in-literature.com/russian-history/

There are movies of great Russian classics such as *Dr. Zhivago, Anna Karenina*, and *War and Peace*, but themes can be very dark. If you wish to watch any of these, I would suggest watching the oldest available versions, as they are likely to treat potentially disturbing scenes less graphically. These are entirely optional, so I will leave it to your discretion as to whether to watch them.

Visual Arts

Make a virtual visit to The Hermitage Museum in St. Petersburg, Russia, where you can see representative samples of Russian art. View the page on Russian and Culture (second link below), and you will be able to explore exhibits of art, clothing, and more. Choose what interests you most—you don't have to look at everything! At the third link, you can take a virtual video tour by selecting a floor, and then clicking on a room, and at the fourth link, you can view panorama photos of various buildings, galleries, and collections.

https://www.hermitagemuseum.org/wps/portal/hermitage/

https://www.hermitagemuseum.org/wps/portal/hermitage/explore/collections/master/1251499791/?lng=en

https://excellence-in-literature.com/hermitage-video-tour/

https://www.hermitagemuseum.org/wps/portal/hermitage/panorama

Use an art history book to look up Russian art. This art is a visual counterpart to the literature in this module, and seeing the connection will help you understand the Russian worldview. You can also see many important paintings at the website below. Just click on links to paintings from at least 12 different artists, and enjoy the variety.

http://webhome.auburn.edu/~mitrege/russian/art/index.html

View the *Russian and the Arts: The Age of Tolstoy and Tchaikovsky* exhibition at the National Portrait Gallery. Read the brief introductions to each section on the page linked below, then look at the portraits. Click the "Tretyakov" link to see the collector who commissioned and donated many of the portraits and if you like, also view the Russian State Tretyakov Gallery linked from the Tretyakov page.

>https://www.npg.org.uk/whatson/russia-and-the-arts/exhibition/portraits

Icons were an early form of Russian art that is very characteristic of the nation. Read this page; then go to the link for "Icons sorted by dates," and look at samples from each century. My favorites are the 15th-century icons of St. George and the Dragon. You may also view the beautiful collections at the Museum of Russian Icons listed below.

>http://copy-www.novsu.ac.ru/novgorod/icon_gallery/english/nig_main.html

>https://www.museumofrussianicons.org

Historical Context

Eyewitness: Russia by Kathleen Berton Murrell is the place to start for a look at the historical context of this module. Look for it at your library or bookstore.

What happened when in Russian history? Although we are focusing on 19th century literature, it can be helpful to understand a bit of the history that shaped the thoughts and writings of the authors you encounter in this module. From the Mongol invasions to the Czarist regimes and on to the revolutionary age of Lenin, Stalin, and communism, Russia's history is both shocking and fascinating.

>https://www.history.com/topics/russia/russia-timeline

>https://excellence-in-literature.com/russian-history/

Bucknell University provides a good resource on Russian history with many links. Get an overview, then browse through the things you find interesting.

>https://www.departments.bucknell.edu/russian/Site-prior-to-Easyweb-migration/chrono.html

>https://www.departments.bucknell.edu/russian/Site-prior-to-Easyweb-migration/history.html

Russia and the Arts

>https://www.npg.org.uk/whatson/russia-and-the-arts/exhibition/portraits

PBS offers "The Face of Russia," an online introduction to Russian history. Look at the timeline section, and click over to the part that covers the 19th century. You can click on images for more information about people and events.

http://www.pbs.org/weta/faceofrussia/intro.html

If it's hard to imagine what it's like to live in a Communist regime, the young reader's book *Breaking Stalin's Nose* by Eugene Yelchin offers a chilling glimpse of the precariousness of life under a totalitarian government. If this interests you, be sure to also read George Orwell's *Animal Farm*, which this curriculum covers in the very first study guide, *Introduction to Literature*.

https://amzn.to/3bGaWhR

https://excellence-in-literature.com/curriculum-user-content/e1-context-resources/eil-1-7-orwell-context/

Places to Go

The Museum of Russian Art is located in Minnesota and is dedicated entirely to Russian art and artifacts. You will find it at 5500 Stevens Ave. South, Minneapolis, MN 55419. If you cannot make it in person, the site offers a photo tour, so be sure to look at that.

https://tmora.org

The Museum of Russian Icons is located in Massachusetts and has the largest collection of its kind in North America. It is at 203 Union Street, Clinton, MA 01510.

https://www.museumofrussianicons.org

The Virginia Museum of Fine Arts is home to a fine collection of the intricately jeweled Fabergé eggs. Many of these beautiful works of art open to reveal tiny surprises. If you can't get there in person, at least view them online.

https://www.vmfa.museum/collections/faberge-and-russian-decorative-arts/

Several of the authors you read in this module have homes still standing in Russia. If you have a chance to travel to that country, search online for [author's name birthplace or home] and you will find at least a few places to visit. If you can't go in person, here are a few online tours.

Pushkin: http://www.saint-petersburg.com/museums/pushkin-museum-memorial-apartment.asp

Tolstoy: https://artsandculture.google.com/story/take-a-tour-through-tolstoy-39-s-home/sgUBH6aQhs50cA?hl=en

Dostoevsky: http://www.saint-petersburg.com/museums/dostoevsky-memorial-museum/ AND http://eng.md.spb.ru

Just for Fun

Technology and classical literature enthusiasts are working together to make Leo Tolstoy's writings available online. Can you imagine proofreading more than 2,000 pages—as a volunteer in your free time?

https://www.newyorker.com/books/page-turner/crowdsourcing-tolstoy

For a charmingly descriptive article about Tolstoy and his country home, read "Count Tolstoy at Home" from an 1891 edition of The Atlantic magazine.

https://www.theatlantic.com/magazine/archive/1891/11/count-tolstoy-at-home/308287/

Assignment Schedule

Week 1

Begin reading the context resources and focus texts. Follow the model in the Formats and Models chapter to write a brief Author Profile for each of the focus text authors in this module. Be sure to refer to your writer's handbook if you have questions about grammar, structure, or style.

Week 2

Write a Historical Period/Event Approach Paper, following the format in the Formats and Models chapter, on the 19th century in Russia and its major events. In addition to the context links I have provided, you may use other resources such as your encyclopedia, the library, and quality Internet resources to complete this assignment.

Week 3

Begin drafting a 750-word paper on one of the topics below. Follow the writing process outlined in the "How to Write an Essay" chapter, consulting the models in the Formats and Models chapter and your writer's handbook as needed.

1- Model: Literary Analysis Essay and MLA Format Model

Prompt: As you read through these works, think back to the 19th-century American and British writers you have read in previous levels of *Excellence in Literature*. How do the lives, experiences, and themes of two or three of these Russian authors compare with their American and British contemporaries? How is this reflected in the art, music, and poetry of each country? Support your thesis with appropriate examples from the texts.

2- Model: Literary Analysis Essay and MLA Format Model

Prompt: Consider what Ivan's prose poem, "The Grand Inquisitor," has to say about free will as opposed to security. What might Dostoevsky be saying about the Russian Orthodox church and how it aligns with the teachings of Christ? After reading "The Grand Inquisitor," which side do you feel Dostoevsky is in agreement with, and how does he use the story to convey this conviction? Be sure to offer specific textual support for your thesis.

3- Model: Literary Analysis Essay and MLA Format Model

Prompt: "The Death of Ivan Ilych" has been seen as a work of moral fiction that is intended to provide moral instruction for its audience. Consider what Tolstoy may have been trying to convey through his story, and consider the ways in which he shows, rather than tells, his audience what he wants them to know or to do. Be sure to offer specific textual support for your thesis.

Week 4

Use the feedback on the rubric, along with the writing mentor's comments, to revise your paper. Before turning in the final draft, be sure you have addressed any issues marked on the evaluation rubric, and verify that the thesis is clear and your essay is well-organized. Use your writer's handbook to check grammar or punctuation so that your essay will be free from mechanical errors. Turn in the essay at the end of the week so that the writing mentor can use the evaluation rubric in the "How to Evaluate" chapter to check your work

Module 5.8

Faust by Johann Wolfgang von Goethe (1749–1832)

If any man wishes to write in a clear style, let him be first clear in his thoughts; and if any would write in a noble style, let him first possess a noble soul.

—Johann Wolfgang von Goethe

Focus Text

Faust by Johann Wolfgang von Goethe

Look for the Norton Critical Edition, as it is an excellent translation with good notes.

Note: This is a challenging book with complex themes, and is generally best reserved for students in 12th grade and above.

Honors Texts

The Screwtape Letters by C. S. Lewis (if you didn't read it in English II) AND

The Picture of Dorian Gray by Oscar Wilde OR

Frankenstein by Mary Shelley OR

Doctor Faustus by Christopher Marlowe

Literary Period

Romantic

Module Focus

In this challenging poetic drama, you will become acquainted with the concept of *Sturm und Drang* and observe how Goethe has adapted an old legend and episodes from mythology into a tale that illustrates Romantic and Enlightenment values.

Introduction

Goethe's *Faust* has been compared in greatness, scope, and power to John Milton's *Paradise Lost*, Dante's *Divine Comedy*, and the works of William Shakespeare. Unlike Milton and Dante, Goethe was not writing from a Christian worldview, but his masterpiece nonetheless speaks a universal truth about what life is like for someone who chooses to sell his or her soul. Because this is a work of fiction, it is not intended for guidance or spiritual instruction.

As the story unfolds, you will see a vivid portrayal of a man who turns away from the light to pursue what he thinks he wants. Satan, in the form of Méphistofélès, offers Faust everything he wants in exchange for his soul. As you can imagine, things go downhill from there. At the end, however . . . well, I will not spoil it for you. Just read or listen carefully, and focus on the contrast between light and darkness.

Something to think about . . .

Early in the drama, Faust is seen in his study. He is preparing to translate the Gospel of John but stops short at the very first sentence, "In the beginning was the Word." He decides this is absurd, and translates *logos* instead as "In the beginning was the deed." What does this tell the reader about Faust's attitude toward Scripture? How does it reflect the Enlightenment value of reason as the primary source for authority?

Be sure to notice . . .

Faust's worship of reason, his pride, and his greed for knowledge cause him to dabble in magic. Does he gain wisdom through doing this? Does he learn anything of value? What are the consequences of his practice?

Context Resources

Readings

Before you begin reading *Faust,* read or listen to the book of *Job* in any translation of the Bible. The two articles linked after the audio version of the Job text discuss some of the parallels and contrasts between the texts. I think you will find them interesting and helpful as you read through this challenging work.

http://www.audiotreasure.com/mp3/18_Job/

https://www.firstthings.com/article/2009/08/hast-thou-considered-my-servant-faust

https://jbqnew.jewishbible.org/assets/Uploads/2/jbq_2_4.pdf

This analytical essay provides the clearest overview I have found of Goethe's *Faust*, and I believe it to be almost essential for understanding the themes of the poem. Although the title mentions a Catholic perspective, this is a literary analysis, not a sectarian or doctrinal statement, and it can also be read as a well-crafted essay model.

https://media.christendom.edu/1996/05/reading-goethes-faust-from-a-catholic-perspective/

Read the definition of "Faustian bargain." Once you know what it is, you will start hearing it in the news and seeing references to it in many situations.

https://www.britannica.com/topic/Faustian-bargain

Look up the meaning of the German literary movement called *Sturm und Drang* in the glossary at the back of this book or online, and watch for examples of it as you read through *Faust*.

https://www.britannica.com/event/Sturm-und-Drang

Dr. Paul Roebuck's website offers a good introduction to this literary movement:

http://web.archive.org/web/20110702041453/http://www.roebuckclasses.com/ideas/sturmunddrang.htm

Read this introduction to literary romanticism from Professor Lilia Melani and the brief overview of the Age of Revolutions. Notice especially the connections between the motivating ideas of both romantics and revolutionaries.

https://excellence-in-literature.com/introduction-to-romanticism-from-lilia-melani/

https://medium.com/traveling-through-history/1774-1849-the-age-of-revolution-a057d4546206

The following articles will give you a good overview of the book and help to keep you oriented as you read.

https://brians.wsu.edu/2016/10/12/goethes-faust/

https://web.archive.org/web/20190911065102/http://faculty.southwest.tn.edu/llipinski/ENGL2320T201/content/lesson18_handout.htm

"The Devil and Daniel Webster" is a short story by Stephen Vincent Benét that plays on the theme of the Faustian bargain. This version has a distinctly American twist.

http://gutenberg.net.au/ebooks06/0602901.txt

The Author's Life

Invitation to the Classics ed. by Cowan and Guinness: If you own or can borrow this book, read the chapter on Goethe (207) and the sections on Western Social and Political Philosophy (190) and German Classics (215).

Online biography of Goethe:

https://excellence-in-literature.com/goethe-biography/

In addition, use the introduction in your copy of *Faust* to gain a greater understanding of Goethe's life and work.

Here are two brief articles: The first discusses Goethe writing process and use of the Faustian legend in his creation of *Faust*, and the second tells of Goethe's cordial meeting with Napoleon Bonaparte.

http://www.theatrehistory.com/german/goethe003.html

http://www.theatrehistory.com/german/goethe008.html

Poetry

Goethe wrote many poems, which you can read in a poetry anthology or online. Be sure to note the Romantic overtones in the tone, subject matter, and style of these poems. The third link below has audio recordings in German, which will help you get the sound of Goethe's poetry in your ears—an important aspect which translation can never fully capture.

Selected Goethe poems, listed mostly by English titles:

https://www.poetryintranslation.com/PITBR/German/Goethepoems.php

Excellent audio recordings of Goethe poems in German with printed English translations:

https://warwick.ac.uk/fac/arts/modernlanguages/about/german-studies/goethe

The highly respected German poet, playwright, and philosopher Friedrich Schiller (1759–1805), sometimes referred to as the German Shakespeare, was one of Goethe's close friends. Here is his poem "Ode to Joy" along with an article on its musical settings by Beethoven and others.

https://r.schillerinstitute.org/transl/schiller_poem/ode_to_joy.pdf

https://archive.schillerinstitute.com/fidelio_archive/1993/fidv02n01-1993Sp/fidv02n01-1993Sp_065-an_early_setting_of_the_ode_to_j.pdf

Optional bio: https://www.newworldencyclopedia.org/entry/Friedrich_Schiller

George Gordon, Lord Byron wrote *Manfred*, a dramatic poem on the Faustian legend.

http://www.bartleby.com/18/6/

Optional: Here is the first part of Byron's *Manfred* with music by Robert Schumann, performed by the Royal Philharmonic Orchestra.

https://youtu.be/757g2bI42NA

Audio

Before you speak of this book to anyone, please listen to the correct pronunciation of the author's last name. It is important to pronounce things correctly!

https://inogolo.com/pronunciation/Goethe

You should be able to find the audiobook of *Faust* at your library or bookstore. At the time of this writing, a free recording is being produced at Librivox.com, so if you do not mind listening to an amateur production with multiple untrained voices, be sure to check if it is available.

https://librivox.org/faust-part-1-by-johann-wolfgang-von-goethe/

Listen to a bit of *Faust* in the original German. It is always useful to know the sound and cadence of other languages. This video shows a few vintage illustrations.

https://excellence-in-literature.com/goethes-faust-read-aloud-video-excerpt/

Music

Franz Liszt wrote a beautiful *Faust* Symphony with three movements. The first is "Faust," the second is "Gretchen," and the third is "Méphistofélès." I have created a playlist with a 1976 Leonard Bernstein performance of this, so you can listen to it as you read through other context materials. Be sure to note the way each character's theme reflects his role, and how the themes of Faust and Méphistofélès change over the course of the symphony as the story unfolds.

https://excellence-in-literature.com/liszts-faust-symphony/

Probably the best known musical works that have been inspired by the story of Faust are two operas: Charles Gounod's *Faust* (1859) and Arrigo Boito's *Mefistofele* (1868). Many other composers have used the drama as a springboard, including Hector Berlioz, Sergei Prokofiev, and Igor Stravinsky, who all composed operas. Ludwig van Beethoven, Franz Schubert, Richard Wagner, Hector Berlioz, Robert Schumann, Franz Liszt, Modest Mussorgsky, and Gustav Mahler were among the composers inspired to write classical music on the theme of Faust. Below are a few recordings and resources, but if you'd like to listen to more, just search for "Faust music" on your favorite streaming service.

This interesting study guide for Gounod's *Faust* provides an outline that will show you how the opera differs from Goethe's story.

https://www.musicwithease.com/gounod-faust.html

Here are performances of *Faust*-inspired pieces. At each page, you will see exactly what composition is being played, and who is playing. Notice the tone and mood of many of these pieces. They are listed here by composer.

Richard Wagner:

https://excellence-in-literature.com/richard-wagner-faust-overture/

This brief analysis of Wagner's overture will help you appreciate it:

https://www.musicwithease.com/wagner-eine-faust-overture.html

Hector Berlioz:

https://excellence-in-literature.com/damnation-of-faust-berlioz

Robert Schumann:

https://excellence-in-literature.com/schumann-faust-overture-music/

Here's a black and white video clip of an opera performance of *Faust*. This is optional, as the images and characters from *Faust* can (and should) be disturbing.

https://excellence-in-literature.com/faust-opera-performance-video-excerpt/

Video

The entire 1926 movie of *Faust* is available with English subtitles. It is a silent film, with music composed and conducted by Timothy Brock and performed by the Olympia Chamber Orchestra. This is interesting, but optional.

https://excellence-in-literature.com/faust-silent-movie-1926/

Visual Arts

Caspar David Friedrich was a German Romantic landscape painter who has been described as one who discovered "the tragedy of landscape." One of his most famous works is "Wanderer above the Sea of Fog." Look at this painting, along with Friedrich's other works and consider how these paintings fit the mood of the Romantic era, and what Friedrich's composition suggests about power.

https://www.caspardavidfriedrich.org

Here is an illustration of Goethe's famous meeting with Napoleon.

http://www.antiquariat-loidl.de/k40/abb/b53408.htm

The mood of romanticism was expressed through the vivid paintings of artist Eugène Delacroix. His work is filled with drama, war, and death, and much of it was inspired by history or literature. The Victoria and Albert Museum in London offers an analytical look at one of his paintings.

http://www.vam.ac.uk/content/articles/o/the-shipwreck-of-don-juan/

It is helpful to view more art from the Romantic era, but rather than searching online, I suggest that you use a young person's art history book such as *The Annotated Mona Lisa* by Carol Strickland, which will provide helpful analysis of individual works in this period.

The dramatic story of *Faust* inspired illustrations by noted artists including Rembrandt, Tissot, Delacroix, and others.

https://excellence-in-literature.com/faust-illustrations/

During Goethe's lifetime, there was an architectural movement known as Gothic Revival. It sought to replace the Neoclassical style of the 17th century with a revival of medieval Gothic style. Look at the images and read the text at the page below, and consider how the style and detail of the buildings might reflect the *sturm und drang* of the Romantic movement.

http://www.essential-architecture.com/STYLE/STY-E05.htm

Historic Context

This illustrated lecture on "The Enlightenment And The Romantic Era" should be helpful to you.

http://loki.stockton.edu/~fergusoc/romantic/romantic.htm

At "Power is never ridiculous!," a teacher at Fort Lauderdale High School in Florida has created an interesting page on the Napoleonic Era, including mention of Napoleon's meeting with Goethe, excerpts from Napoleon's diary, and a couple of cartoons of the day.

http://www.thecaveonline.com/APEH/napoleon.html

The Enlightenment: This was a time in which worldviews about authority, epistemology, and the nature of man changed. Read about this historic period to help you understand why knowledge and reason were so important to Goethe, and by extension, to Faust.

https://brians.wsu.edu/2016/10/12/the-enlightenment/

During the Enlightenment, a long-distance intellectual community flourished in Europe and the Americas. You may read about the "Republic of Letters" below.

https://www.neh.gov/humanities/2013/novemberdecember/feature/mapping-the-republic-letters

Optional: This article offers a look at Enlightenment values and their social and political implications over the last two centuries.

https://www.catholicculture.org/culture/library/view.cfm?recnum=7805

Places to Go

You may take a quick online tour of Goethe's home in Frankfurt Germany, or go there in person if you have the chance. To take the online tour, click on each floor, then on the individual rooms.

https://frankfurter-goethe-haus.de/en/

Just for Fun

French poet Gérard de Nerval translated *Faust* from German into French when he was only 20 years old. He may have been a genius, but he was also noted for walking his pet lobster, Thibault, on a ribbon in Paris's Palais Royale garden.

Assignment Schedule

Week 1

Begin reading the context resources and the novel, and follow the model in the Formats and Models chapter to write an Author Profile. Be sure to refer to your writer's handbook if you have questions about grammar, structure, or style.

Week 2

When you finish the novel, write an Approach Paper on the novel. You will find the format and a sample paper in the Formats and Models chapter. In addition to the context links in this module, you may use other resources such as your encyclopedia, the library, and quality Internet resources to complete this assignment.

Alternative Assignment

In the first part of the drama, Faust listens to Méphistoféles' proposal. Imagine that you are a neighbor or friend of Faust, and you have his best interests at heart. Write him a letter warning of the perils of making a pact with Satan, and suggest a better way to find lasting joy and happiness. Make this as long as it needs to be in order to persuade Faust not to make this foolish choice.

Week 3

Begin drafting a 750-word paper on one of the topics below. I recommend that you follow the writing process outlined in the "How to Write an Essay" chapter, consulting the models in the Formats and Models chapter and your writer's handbook as needed.

1- Model: Literary Analysis Essay and MLA Format Model

Prompt: In Homer's *Odyssey*, Odysseus is the archetypal hero on a quest. Compare and contrast the journeys of Odysseus and Faust, their motivations, the dangers and temptations they encounter, and the most important lesson each man learns during his travel through life. Be sure to support your thesis with appropriate quotes from the text.

2- Model: Literary Analysis Essay and MLA Format Model

Prompt: If the entire drama is a commentary on what happens to someone who turns away from God, what does Goethe seem to be saying about this choice? Did Faust's choice bring him what he wanted? How can it be compared to the fall of Adam in Genesis? Be sure to support your thesis with appropriate quotes from the text.

3- Model: Literary Analysis Essay and MLA Format Model

Prompt—Advanced topic: Essay author John Whiton suggests that

> Goethe's protagonist undergoes a development taking him beyond Idealism to an essentially Realist understanding of the world, but a Realism which goes beyond Aristotle to see that creation is in a profound sense symbolic, or, in an analogous sense, sacramental; and that fulfillment comes not from the hubris of unbridled self-realization but rather from a humble acceptance of the human condition as a given.

Whiton Essay: https://media.christendom.edu/1996/05/reading-goethes-faust-from-a-catholic-perspective/

Evaluate this thesis in light of your own reading of *Faust*, and discuss Faust's development, considering Faust's original goals and how his relationship with Méphistoféles evolved over the course of the book. You may agree or disagree with Whiton's argument, but you must support your analysis with evidence from the text and the essay.

Week 4

Use the feedback on the rubric, along with the writing mentor's comments, to revise your paper. Before turning in the final draft, fix any issues marked on the evaluation rubric. Use your writer's handbook to check grammar, style, and usage so that your essay will be free from simple errors. Turn in the essay at the end of the week so that the writing mentor can use the evaluation rubric in the "How to Evaluate" chapter to check your work.

Module 5.9

Out of Africa by Isak Dinesen (1885-1962)

When you have a great and difficult task, something perhaps almost impossible,
if you only work a little at a time, every day a little, suddenly the work will finish itself.
—Isak Dinesen

Focus Text

Out of Africa by Isak Dinesen, a pseudonym for Baroness Karen von Blixen-Finecke

"Babette's Feast" by Isak Dinesen (a short story)

Honors Text

Cry the Beloved Country by Alan Paton

Surprised by Joy: The Shape of My Early Life by C.S. Lewis

Literary Period

Modernist Period/Romantic Style

Module Focus

In this module you will learn about the conventions of writing memoir, and see how it differs from autobiography.

Introduction

Out of Africa is Danish writer Karen von Blixen's evocative memoir of a now-vanished time and place. Although Kenya exists, Isak Dinesen's farm in Africa has been divided and developed, so her personal world no longer exists as she knew it, though it continues to exist within her book. Her short story, "Babette's Feast," also speaks of beauty and loss within a completely different context. Dinesen writes beautifully, and her work powerfully captures and conveys shades of meaning and mood. She wrote during the Modernist era, but her work is in the Romantic tradition.

During Dinesen's life, she knew many famous people, and her work was immensely popular. When Ernest Hemingway accepted the Nobel Prize in 1954, he said, "As a Nobel Prize winner I cannot but regret that the award was never given to Mark Twain, nor to Henry James, speaking only of my own countrymen. Greater writers than these also did not receive the prize. I would have been happy—happier—today if the prize had been given to that beautiful writer Isak Dinesen . . . " (Excerpted from *The New York Times Book Review*, November 7, 1954). This is high praise indeed from one of the great writers of the 20th century. In the final analysis, it is Dinesen's beautiful prose and unique perspective that make her memoir and her stories unforgettable.

Something to think about . . .

Denmark is an old, old country, with a history that goes back many centuries. Its traditions are filled with myth, legend, and folklore. Like other Scandinavian countries, Denmark has been mostly secular for many years, with nearly half its citizens identifying themselves as atheists or agnostics. As you read *Out of Africa* and "Babette's Feast," read also Psalm 19:1-4, and consider what you discern about Dinesen's attitude toward creation.

Be sure to notice . . .

Isak Dinesen identified herself a storyteller, and her most noted works were vivid short stories. How does she use storytelling and storytelling techniques throughout *Out of Africa* to evoke a strong feeling of time and place? What do the storytelling techniques achieve that could not be achieved by the more structured outline of an autobiography? How does memoir differ from autobiography, and why do you think Dinesen chose this form for her memories of the farm in Africa?

Context Resources

Readings

Paul Gregory Alms offers some thoughts on the memoir and postmodernism, in contrast to the art of biography and modernism. This brief essay may help you to put Dinesen's memoir in context.

https://excellence-in-literature.com/memoir-as-post-modern-history/

"Kierkegaard at Babette's Feast: The Return to the Finite" by Jean Schuler is an excellent article from the Journal of Religion and Film. Click on "Download" to read the entire article after you have read "Babette's Feast."

https://digitalcommons.unomaha.edu/jrf/vol1/iss2/3/

The Danish existentialist philosopher Søren Kierkegaard is said to be one of Isak Dinesen's major influences. Read about him at the first two links, and one of his philosophical essays at the second link.

https://www.britannica.com/biography/Soren-Kierkegaard

https://www.christianitytoday.com/history/people/moversandshakers/soren-kierkegaard.html

https://formeraspiringphilosopher.com/2015/12/14/the-king-the-maiden-kierkegaards-christmas-parable/

"Babette's Feast: A Fable for Culinary France" is an excerpt from Priscilla Parkhurst Ferguson's *Accounting for Taste: The Triumph of French Cuisine*. This chapter discusses both the short story and the movie, and offers significant analysis of the ideas and events in the story. You may find the book at the library, or read this chapter online. Note: The word "sensuality" as used in this chapter may be defined as "the condition of being pleasing or fulfilling to the senses."

https://press.uchicago.edu/Misc/Chicago/243230.html

One Thousand and One Arabian Nights by Geraldine McCaughrean: Dinesen speaks of storytelling throughout *Out of Africa*, occasionally mentioning the stories of *1001 Arabian Nights*. This piece of classic literature obviously influenced her writing. You may read from the original version, or look for this well-written young people's translation in the library or bookstore, and read the framing narrative and at least a few of the stories so that you will understand the references in the focus text. Remember that the framing narrative is the story that provides a framework for the other stories—in this case, it is the story of a young woman who keeps herself alive by telling a story every night.

https://amzn.to/3pbrvHW

The Merchant of Venice by William Shakespeare: Get familiar with the plot of this play, so that you can understand the discussion between Dinesen and Farah.

https://absoluteshakespeare.com/guides/summaries/merchant_of_venice/merchant_of_venice_summary.htm

Don't miss Josh Gibbs' excellent article, "Babette's Feast and the Beatific Vision." It will help to orient you within the story.

https://excellence-in-literature.com/babettes-feast-the-beatific-vision/

The Author's Life

Look for Roger Leslie's *Isak Dinesen: Gothic Storyteller,* part of the outstanding Writers of Imagination series. If you cannot find, it, another middle-grade biography or an encyclopedia source is acceptable.

https://amzn.to/3uEjDQv

The Karen Blixen Museum offers a look at the author's life, work, and time in Africa. Be sure to look at the illustrated timeline of her life and consider what else was happening in the world during her lifetime.

https://blixen.dk/en/karen-blixen/karen-blixens-life

The Paris Review has published an interesting interview with Dinesen. You may not be able to access the entire thing, but read as much as you can.

https://www.theparisreview.org/interviews/4911/the-art-of-fiction-no-14-isak-dinesen

What was Kenya like when Isak Dinesen/Karen Blixen lived there? "In Search of Karen Blixen's Kenya" from the New York Times will help you visual her world.

https://www.nytimes.com/1986/01/12/travel/in-search-of-karen-blixen-s-kenya.html

Poetry

A. E. Housman was a poet that both Isak Dinesen and Denys Finch-Hatton enjoyed and quoted. Read "To An Athlete Dying Young" and the other poems at the page below.

https://excellence-in-literature.com/a-e-housman-poetry/

Rainer Maria Rilke

Biography: https://poets.org/poet/rainer-maria-rilke

Poems: https://excellence-in-literature.com/rainer-maria-rilke-poetry/

Marianne Moore

Biography: https://poets.org/poet/marianne-moore

Poems: https://excellence-in-literature.com/marianne-moore-poetry/

Audio

You should be able to find the audiobook of *Out of Africa* at your library or bookstore. It is not yet in the public domain, so you will not find it online except in illegal pirated versions.

http://amzn.to/2rV4LOn

Music

Dinesen enjoyed classical music, including opera. Mozart's opera, *The Marriage of Figaro*, is a good example of what she would have heard. The YouTube link below offers a full-length recording of an entire performance with subtitles. If you are unable to access it for some reason, just search the site for another performance or listen to the piano excerpts below.

https://youtu.be/_OYtlGpApco

You may listen to piano excerpts from *The Marriage of Figaro*, at the "Opera in a Nutshell" site. Just click on the links for "Le Nozze di Figaro" to listen.

http://www.impresario.ch/opera/nuce/nutmoz.htm

The soundtrack for *Out of Africa* has beautiful and evocative music. Get it from your library or bookstore, and listen to it as you study. You can hear an excerpt at the link below.

https://excellence-in-literature.com/out-of-africa-soundtrack-music/

Video

There is a 1985 movie of *Out of Africa*. I saw it when it first came out and recall a great deal of beautiful scenery, but not much else. Please consult a reliable guide in order to decide whether it is suitable for your family.

"Babette's Feast" has been made into a beautiful film. You may view a parental guide for it at http://www.imdb.com/title/tt0092603/parentalguide in order to decide whether to view it. I did not find anything objectionable about it, but you will wish to make the decision for yourself.

Visual Arts

Isak Dinesen highly valued art and even studied painting for a time. She writes that

> I have always had difficulty seeing how a landscape looked, if I had not first got the key to it from a great painter. I have experienced and recognized a land's particular character where a painter has interpreted it to me. Constable, Gainsborough and Turner showed me England. When I travelled to Holland as a young girl, I understood all that the landscape and the cities said because the old Dutch painters did me the kind service of interpreting it; and in the Umbrian blueness around Perugia I was, by the hands of Giotto and Fra Angelico, quietly blessed." Quoted in *Isak Dinesen: The Life of a Storyteller* by Judith Thurman.

You may view a few of the paintings by artists who were part of Dinesen's experience.

https://excellence-in-literature.com/british-artists/

https://excellence-in-literature.com/italian-artists/

https://excellence-in-literature.com/dutch-masters/

Here is a site with information about the setting for the movie of "Babette's Feast." Click on the link for "Maarup Church" to see a photo of the church used in the filming—this will give you an impression of the Danish landscape that Isak Dinesen knew. This ancient Romanesque church was built c.1250 at the edge of a cliff that has since eroded. The church was partially dismantled in 2008.

http://www.karenblixen.com/question50.html

Visit the library or a bookstore, and look in the travel section for books on Kenya and Denmark. Look at the photographs, and compare Dinesen's two landscapes. Notice how well her prose captures the visual mood of each country.

Historic Context

A professor at Emory University has posted a good overview of Isak Dinesen and her work in a Colonial context, including a section on the controversy over her view of the natives.

https://scholarblogs.emory.edu/postcolonialstudies/2014/06/10/207/

Historian Bamber Gascoigne offers a helpful overview of Kenyan history. I suggest supplementing this with a look at a world atlas to view maps of the region.

https://excellence-in-literature.com/history-of-kenya-by-bamber-gascoigne/

Please refer to your encyclopedia or a library resource to see maps and read more about colonialism, Kenya, and Denmark.

Places to Go

The Karen Blixen Museum in Denmark is located in Rungstedlund, the house where she lived as a child, and returned to as an adult.

https://blixen.dk/en/visit-the-museum

You will also find a Karen Blixen Museum in Nairobi, Kenya. It was set up in M'Bogani House, the main building of Blixen's coffee farm at the foot of the Ngong Hills.

https://www.museums.or.ke/karen-blixen/

Assignment Schedule

Week 1

Begin reading the context resources and the novel, and follow the model in the Formats and Models chapter to write an Author Profile. Be sure to refer to your writer's handbook if you have questions about grammar, structure, or style.

Week 2

For each of the five sections of *Out of Africa*, choose an episode and retell it in some way. You may write a news story in journalistic format, write a poem, draw it as a graphic story (cartoon panel style as in the *Tin-Tin* books), or assume a character in the book, and write a letter or journal entry from that perspective and voice. You will have five retellings of various lengths when you finish.

Week 3

Begin drafting a 750-word paper on one of the topics below. I recommend that you follow the writing process outlined in the "How to Write an Essay" chapter, consulting the models in the Formats and Models chapter and your writer's handbook as needed.

1- Model: Literary Analysis Essay and MLA Format Model

Prompt: Isak Dinesen always chose to identify herself as a storyteller. Discuss ways in which her memoir, *Out of Africa*, is an example of storytelling, and how it is different from an autobiography. Be sure to support your thesis with appropriate examples from the text.

2- Model: Literary Analysis Essay and MLA Format Model

Prompt: Isak Dinesen told stories to the native people and enjoyed their responses. When she related the story of Shakespeare's *Merchant of Venice* to Farah, what does his response reveal about the differences between European and native cultures? How do these differences affect the way we read books from another culture, and how can literature help to build understanding between cultures? Be sure to use quotes from the text and your research to support your thesis.

Week 4

Use the feedback on the rubric, along with the writing mentor's comments, to revise your paper. Before turning in the final draft, be sure you have addressed any issues marked on the evaluation rubric, and verify that the thesis is clear and your essay is well-organized. Use your writer's handbook to check grammar or punctuation so that your essay will be free from mechanical errors. Turn in the essay at the end of the week so that the writing mentor can use the evaluation rubric in the "How to Evaluate" chapter to check your work.

Honors

Start writing, no matter what. The water does not flow until the faucet is turned on.
— Louis L'Amour

Key components of the Honors Option (in addition to regular assignments related to the focus text) include reading, writing, a final project, and an optional final exam.

- Reading: Usually one extra novel, play, or epic poem.
- Writing: An approach paper unless otherwise directed.
- Final project: One 6- to 10-page research paper (depending on student's grade level).
- CLEP test for some levels.

Extra Reading

Honors reading for each module is listed within the module. Each item has been chosen to coordinate in some way with the focus of the module. It might be an additional work by the focus text author or one of his/her contemporaries or something that is related in subject matter, theme, or genre.

Since the Honors option essentially doubles the reading load, you may need to think creatively about scheduling. You might finish the focus text during the first two weeks of the module and the Honors text in the last two weeks, or you might save a few of the texts to read as summer reading or between semesters.

Approach Papers

For one full-length honors text per module, you should complete an approach paper unless an alternative assignment is recommended. If more than one honors text is suggested with "AND" you would read both texts. If it's suggested with "OR", you may choose which to read and which to use as the subject for the approach paper. It is not necessary to write more than one honors approach paper per module.

Summary Titles

For each of the texts you read, create summary titles for each chapter or scene. A summary title is just what it sounds like—a title that summarized the contents or at least the main point of the chapter. This was common in the 18th and 19th centuries, as it gave potential readers a hint of what was coming. For novels that first appeared in serialized form, a summary title not only reminded readers of major characters and events in the story, it could also entice new readers to become interested. Here are some examples of summary titles from two of the books you will read in EIL.

From *Around the World in Eighty Days* by Jules Verne:

> Chapter XI: In Which Phileas Fogg Secures a Curious Means of Conveyance at a Fabulous Price
>
> Chapter XIV: In Which Phileas Fogg Descends The Whole Length Of The Beautiful Valley Of The Ganges Without Ever Thinking Of Seeing It
>
> Chapter XXII: In Which Passepartout Finds Out That, Even At The Antipodes, It Is Convenient To Have Some Money In One's Pocket

From *Don Quixote* by Miguel de Cervantes:

> Chapter VIII: Of The Good Fortune Which The Valiant Don Quixote Had In The Terrible And Undreamt-Of Adventure Of The Windmills, With Other Occurrences Worthy To Be Fitly Recorded
>
> Chapter L Wherein Is Set Forth Who The Enchanters And Executioners Were Who Flogged The Duenna And Pinched Don Quixote, And Also What Befell The Page Who Carried The Letter To Teresa Panza, Sancho Panza's Wife

Like these examples, the summary titles you write should concisely summarize the contents of the chapter or scene in the most interesting way possible. Your summary titles can be helpful if you end up writing about the book in your research paper, but more importantly, these brief chapter or scene summaries will form a complete summary of the whole book and will help you remember what happened, including when, where, how, and why.

Research Paper Topic and Due Date

A research paper will be due two weeks after the end of the spring semester. The topic will be your choice of one of the authors you have studied this year. You can choose from the focus or Honors text authors, or even one of the poets that you read during the year. Your paper length will vary, depending on which EIL level you are in.

Format

— Length: E1–6 pages; E2–7 pages; E3–8 pages; E4–9 pages; E5–10 pages.

Your paper should be submitted in MLA format, the same format you have been using for essays. You will find more information about formatting in Section 9 (page 408) of the EIL *Handbook for Writers*, and at the OWL link below. Be sure to include a Works Cited page with a minimum of four resources. Up to two of the resources may be Internet sources chosen in accordance with accepted academic standards. You will find detailed, step-by-step instructions for researching, writing, and documenting your research paper at Purdue University's Online Writing Lab (OWL)

https://owl.purdue.edu/owl/general_writing/common_writing_assignments/research_papers/index.html

Suggestions for the Author Research Paper

A research paper has been described as a thoughtful inquiry into a topic you find interesting. You will find detailed instructions in most writer's handbooks for how to do research, keep track of sources, list citations, format your research paper, and so forth. Once you have decided on the author who will be the focus of your Honors paper, here are things you may want to include:

- overview of the author's life;
- people, groups, and events that influenced the author's life and writing;
- overview of the author's body of work and his or her reputation among peers and in the general public;
- analysis of one or more of the author's best- or least-known works;
- how the author's work has influenced later writers or a genre of literature.

CLEP Test

If you have chose the Honors option, your final exam, which can be taken at the end of the school year, will be a CLEP test. Many colleges and universities grant advanced placement and/or college credit (up to six credits) for a passing score on these exams, so it is well worth the effort. (I earned forty-five credits toward my B.A. by taking exams on subjects I had studied on my own.)

These 90-minute, multiple-choice, computer-based exams can be taken by appointment at a local college or community college. Learn more about each exam, including what percentages of each exam are devoted to particular topics, and get practice materials at clep.collegeboard.org.

Suggested Schedule for CLEP Exams		
EIL Year	Suggested Exam	What it Covers
After E1, Introduction to Literature	Analyzing and Interpreting Literature* https://clep.collegeboard.org/composition-and-literature/analyzing-and-interpreting-literature	This skills-based exam focuses on questions about passages from American and British literature.
After E2, Literature and Composition	College Composition* https://clep.collegeboard.org/composition-and-literature/college-composition	This exam evaluates skills taught in most first-year college writing courses.
After E3, American Literature	American Literature https://clep.collegeboard.org/composition-and-literature/american-literature	This broad, general survey exam focuses on American literature from colonial time to the present.
After E4, British Literature	English Literature https://clep.collegeboard.org/composition-and-literature/english-literature	This broad, general survey exam focuses on major British authors and literary works.
After E5, World Literature	Humanities https://clep.collegeboard.org/composition-and-literature/humanities	This exam evaluates knowledge of literature, art, and music and other performing arts.

*Option: The first two exams are skills-based exams, so you may wait to take them until you have done three or more years of EIL and other high school writing. The more practice you have, the better you are likely to score. The other three exams include knowledge-based questions, so it's best to take them right after the year of study is completed.

Tips for Writing a College-Ready Research Paper

You can find detailed instructions for planning and writing a research paper at Purdue University's Online Writing Lab and over 100 pages of instruction in the "Essays and Arguments" section in the Excellence in Literature *Handbook for Writers*, but what those instructions don't tell you is how to take your paper from snooze-worthy to spectacular. These seven tips will help you do it.

1: Know What is Expected

First, get acquainted with the assignment details. One of the best ways to do this is to copy the assignment into your brainstorming notebook and note any specific formatting requirements. Copying forces you to slow down and pay attention, and it can help you begin to discover resources and think through the topic.

2: Take Charge of Your Topic

Once you know what is expected, define your focus. It is both easier and more interesting to write in depth about a narrow topic than to offer a superficial look at a large topic. Here are two examples of how you might narrow the focus of a general topic.

History Example

General Subject: The French Revolution

Overall Focus: The general causes of the French Revolution

Narrow Focus: The social and political causes of the French Revolution

Narrower Focus: The immediate cause: the economic problem

Literature Example

General Subject: Hamlet by William Shakespeare

Overall Focus: Women in the play

Narrow Focus: A woman in the play: Ophelia

Narrower Focus: Ophelia's relationship with her father

Narrowest Focus: The scene in which Ophelia and Polonius first discuss Hamlet (Act I, Scene 3).

3: Start an Argument

A paper without an argument often sounds like a rewrite of a Wikipedia entry, so in order to take your paper to the next level, state an opinion in the thesis. This not only makes your paper more compelling, it also makes it easier to write. In the following example, consider the difference between a simple statement without an argument, and the more closely-focused thesis that provides a clear opinion to defend.

Statement: "Polonius is Ophelia's father, and when he dies, she goes insane."

Thesis with an argument: "Polonius's treatment of his daughter reveals a poisonous emotional climate at Elsinore, and suggests that his attitude and political ambitions are the source of much of the evil in the court."

Arguments belong in all types of research papers, including science and history. For example, if you are assigned a paper about Galileo, and you decide to focus on his astronomical observations, you wouldn't write an encyclopedia-style entry describing his work. For an outstanding paper, you might begin with an argument such as, "Galileo's astronomical observations were a breakthrough that effectively challenged the traditional views of the universe and introduced a bold new method of understanding the heavens." You could support this by offering evidence related to his observations, methods, and the traditional views challenged by his work. The strong, focused, argument-based thesis provides a foundation for everything that follows.

4: Craft an Orderly Introduction

The introduction of the paper will introduce your reader to the subject and focus of your paper, engage interest, and outline your thesis. The introduction to a spectacular research paper might follow the following model.

1. In the opening sentence, announce the general subject (piracy, a particular work of literature, a political event, a social issue, and so on). The general subject matter will often be contained in the essay topic your instructor has provided.

2. In the next two or three sentences, narrow the focus to one particular aspect of that general subject, so the reader understands that you are not dealing with all questions arising from that subject but only with one particular question or area of concern.

3. Finally in the last one or two sentences at the end of the introduction, define the thesis by announcing your opinion about that focus so that the reader understands what you are arguing.

5: Draw a Line of Evidence

Once the argument is introduced, establish a line of linked evidence that leads logically to the conclusion. Begin by brainstorming all the points you might want to discuss. Select evidence that most strongly supports the thesis, and write a topic sentence for each selected point. Topic sentences must argue only one piece of evidence, which will be supported in the balance of the paragraph. Create a topic sentence outline by arranging the topic sentences in the most persuasive order.

6: Make Every Paragraph Pull its Weight

In a spectacular research paper, every paragraph is made up of strong sentences that advance the argument in some way. Each paragraph should discuss one supporting point, and provide substantial evidence for that point alone. An excellent paragraph should include:

1. Topic sentence, an assertion announcing the main point of the paragraph, perhaps followed by one or two sentences reinforcing and clarifying the argumentative stance in this paragraph;

2. Evidence in the form of direct references to the text, quotations, statistics, summaries of relevant research data, and so on.

3. Interpretation of the evidence, a section which discusses in detail how the particular evidence you have introduced helps to back up the argumentative point announced in the topic sentence;

4. (Optional) Any qualifications you want to introduce to limit the argument, and especially to clarify the reliability of the evidence and thus the interpretations you have made of it;

5. Final summary point bringing the reader back to the point stressed in the topic sentence.

7: Wrap it Tightly

By the time you reach the end of your excellent research paper, the reader should have no doubt about the focus of the paper and the scope of your argument. Your concluding paragraph should wrap up your argument with a compelling summary of the evidence. If appropriate for your topic, you could also look ahead or suggest a course of action based upon the thesis.

As you work through your paper, read it aloud to yourself. Listen to see if sentences make sense and are gracefully linked. Once the final draft is complete, read it aloud to someone else and ask for feedback on its clarity, structure, and flow. Writing a strong research paper takes time, but with a focused topic, strong argument, and carefully organized and presented evidence, your paper can move to the head of the class.

Note: Examples adapted from the Excellence in Literature *Handbook for Writers*, available at Writers-Handbook.com.

Formats and Models

Read, read, read. Read everything—trash, classics, good and bad, and see how they do it.
Just like a carpenter who works as an apprentice and studies the master.
Read! You'll absorb it. Then write.
If it's good, you'll find out. If it's not, throw it out of the window..
— William Faulkner

There is a long and honorable tradition of using models or samples to learn to write well. The formats and models are you find here will help you understand the elements of each kind of assignment you will do. Each basic type of paper practiced in EIL is presented with a "Format"—instructions for what each paper should contain—plus a "Model"—a student-written sample of what a completed paper might look like. These models have been used with the permission of some of my former students and are examples of what each type of assignment should contain when it is turned in.

The final paper in this section is a general model of an essay written in MLA format with examples of how to integrate and format quotations of prose or poetry. This model will be useful for all your Week 3 writing assignments.

In every assignment, please use MLA format (see the final model in this section, titled "MLA Format Model"). Remember to put your name, the date, the class name, and the module number and focus text title in the top left corner of each assignment you turn in. For essays or stories, also copy the assignment prompt just below this information so that you will have it handy as you are writing, and your evaluator will know exactly what question you are answering.

Note to Parents About the Model Papers

When you look at these papers, please do not panic. They are the work of some of my best students over the years, and they offer a look at what is possible, not necessarily what is routinely expected. Also, please do not assume that a student's interpretation in the sample paper is the "right" one. It is simply that student's impression. Your student's paper may be quite different, and that is perfectly fine as long as his or her opinions are backed up by evidence (quotes) from the text. As for writing quality, if your student is not yet producing work of this caliber, be patient. With each completed assignment you will see growth and improvement, and that incremental growth is what you will build on. You don't have to start at the top to have good results; you just need to climb steadily!

Approach Paper Format

One of my favorite tools for literary analysis is the approach paper. Although "approach paper" may seem to be an odd name for an analytical assignment, it makes sense when you realize that the exercise of writing each section of the approach paper helps to guide your thinking as you approach the essay assignment.

An approach paper consists of several sections:

I. **MLA-style heading** with your name, date, class, and name of the work you will be analyzing. (See sample for proper format.)

II. **Summary Paragraph:** A three- or four-sentence paragraph that summarizes the book or other work in as much descriptive detail as possible. Each of the sentences in your summary must begin in a different way, and sentences should be varied in length and full of interesting detail. If you need help with this, the *Handbook for Writers* provides guidance in how to form and style sentences and paragraphs, plus guidance for issues of grammar, style and usage. The summary is sometimes the most difficult section of the approach paper to write because it takes time to condense the events of a whole novel, play, or epic poem into just a few well-written sentences.

III. **Character Descriptions:** Choose and list three or four main characters in the work you are studying. In just four or five adjectives, vividly describe the character. This might be a good time to use some of the new or unusual vocabulary words you've encountered in the book, or to check the dictionary and thesaurus for ideas. Descriptive words may be used only once per approach paper, so if you use a word to describe one character, you may not use the same word to describe another character.

IV. **Discussion/Essay Questions:** Write three questions about the novel, poem, play, or essay. These questions should be thought-provoking and will almost always take more than one line to type because they ask readers to combine more than one idea. They must not be questions of fact, but of interpretation, just like the questions that are provided for your essay assignments. The act of writing this type of question helps you to think more insightfully about the characters in relationship to one another and to the setting, the author's style and intention, and the voice and reliability of the narrator. When you think seriously about these issues, you begin to approach an understanding of the text.

V. **Key Passage:** Choose the passage you feel is the most important passage in the work. This may be a brief paragraph, or it may be an entire page or more. Type it up word-for-word in the approach paper. Be sure to identify the speakers if the passage includes dialogue.

VI. **Key Passage Explanation:** In a fully developed paragraph, explain why your chosen passage is important to understanding the focus text. In your explanation make sure you integrate quotes (actual words or phrases) from the key passage to strengthen your explanation, using proper MLA format as demonstrated in your handbook or in the sample essay in this guide. Often, your chosen key passage will offer clues to the novel, poem, or play's themes. If you notice this, be sure to mention it in your explanation.

Approach Paper Model

Student's Name

Date

English V: Instructor's Name

Don Quixote Approach Paper

Summary:

  Don Quixote by Miguel de Cervantes is the classic tale of a Spanish madman named Don Quixote, who decides to become a knight. Along with his devoted squire Sancho Panza, Don Quixote forces himself and others into undesirable adventures throughout the Spanish nation of Castille. But Don Quixote also finds that the world does not desire a return to the old world of chivalry, for he is scorned at every turn for his desire to revive a long-lost golden age of Europe. On two different occasions, in fact, a bachelor named Sansón Carrasco (disguised as a knight-errant) tries to defeat the deluded knight in jousts, attempting to order him to return to his hometown in La Mancha. On the second attempt, Sansón defeats Don Quixote, and grants him life under the condition that he return to his home and forsake the order of knight-errantry. After Don Quixote returns home, he regains his sanity and declares, "I now abhor all profane stories of knight-errantry."

Characters

- Sancho Panza: gullible, subservient, opportunistic, acquisitive
- Don Quixote: quixotic*, idealistic, chimerical, fatuous, psychotic
- Sansón Carrasco: covetous, arrogant, avaricious, pugnacious

Discussion Questions

- The characters in *Don Quixote* make numerous references to Miguel de Cervantes himself, as though the author were a contemporary of the characters. How is the author's opinion about himself portrayed in the book? What attributes of Cervantes' own life and philosophy are expressed within the characters?
- Much of the parody in *Don Quixote* is affected by the unusual combination between knight-errantry and sixteenth-century life. How do the civilizations of Amadis of Gaul and King Arthur of England differ from Don Quixote's world?

- Cervantes makes many references to the relationship between Moors and Christians in sixteenth-century Spain. Has the relationship changed since the age when the Moors were driven out of Spain? If so, how?

Key Passage, from Chapter XV of Book II, p. 627

In his first joust with Sansón Carrasco, Don Quixote emerges victorious from battle and elated with joy over his triumph. Afterward, the following passage ensues:

> Carrasco undertook the task [to defeat Don Quixote in a joust], and Tomé Cecial, Sancho's comrade and neighbor, a merry, scatterbrained fellow, offered his services as squire. Sansón armed himself as has been described and Tomé Cecial, to avoid being recognized by his comrade when they met, fitted on over his natural nose the false one already mentioned. And so they followed the same road as Don Quixote and very nearly reached him in time to be present at the adventure of the cart of Death, and at last they met in the wood, where everything that the extraordinary fancies of Don Quixote, who took it into his head that the bachelor was not the bachelor, Master Bachelor licentiate, because he did not find nests where he expected to find birds. Tomé Cecial, seeing how badly their plans had turned out and what a wretched end their expedition had come to, said to the bachelor: "For sure, Master Sansón Carrasco, we've met with our deserts. It is easy to plan and start an enterprise, but most times it is hard to get out of it safe and sound. Don Quixote is mad, and we are sane, but he comes off safe and in high spirits, while you, master, are left drubbed and downcast. Tell us, now, who is the greater madman, he who is so because he cannot help it, or he who is so of his own free will?"

Key Passage Explanation:

This passage offers a panoramic view of the whole paradox of Don Quixote. Don Quixote is mad, but the sane madness of his opponents is even worse, for in their depravity they are mad of their "own free will." We see in this passage that everyone is a sort of villain in this book. Don Quixote meets with his own hardships, but as Tomé Cecial points out, "We've met with our own deserts [deserved punishments]." Cervantes does not advocate the false chivalry promulgated in the books of knight-errantry, but neither does he support its alternative. By ridiculing both extremes, Cervantes tacitly expresses his desire for a balance.

Historical Approach Paper Format

Event or Era

Place

Time

Event Summary

Write an interesting one-paragraph summary of the period or event.

Key Players

Choose 3–4 key people involved in the event, and list 4–5 vividly descriptive words for each person. Words may not be used to describe more than one character.

Discussion Questions

Think carefully about the event, and write three analytical discussion questions.

Turning Point

Choose an event that seems to mark a significant turning point or climax in the period or event, and write a one-paragraph description.

Turning Point Explanation

Why do you believe this was a significant turning point? What happened afterward? Write a fully developed paragraph explaining your choice. Support your argument with quotes from the text or other sources, if appropriate.

Historical Approach Paper Model

Student's Name

Date

English I: Instructor's Name

Event: Russian Revolution

Place: Russia

Time: 1917

Event/Era Summary

The Russian Revolution was not a single event in which Tsar Nicholas II was defeated and removed from power, but a broad expression of two events, the February

Revolution and the October Revolution. Leading up to the February Revolution, Russia experienced turmoil and political conflict over issues such as the country's economic condition and its prevailing failure in World War I. Conditions in Russia continued to worsen until a festival in one of Russia's prominent cities turned into a large protest, inducing Nicholas II to order a military intervention which proved futile, as much of his military was no longer loyal. This event caused Nicholas II to resign the position of tsar to his brother, Michael Alexandrovich, who was not willing to serve without election. Without anyone to fill the position, Russia had no other choice than to set up a temporary government, eventually headed by Alexander Kerensky. Another important character, Vladimir Lenin, plays a significant role in the October Revolution as a member of the communist revolution with a plan to overthrow the current government. Lenin's plan worked to perfection as military guards laid down their arms immediately without resistance. Alexander Kerensky soon fled the palace and the new government, led by Lenin, took effect.

Key Players

- Tsar Nicholas II: obstinate, neglectful, destructive, intelligent
- Vladimir Lenin: persuasive, radical, visionary, rebellious
- Alexander Kerensky: popular, successful, convincing, renowned

Discussion Questions

I. Though it may have been due to his lack of political education, Nicholas II made many mistakes as a leader. What measures could he have taken in an attempt to avoid the widespread upheaval that occurred?

II. Why was Vladimir Lenin so successful in spreading the principles of Marxism? Did the people find hope in his ideas when it seemed as if there was no hope?

III. How did conditions change in Russia after the Revolution of 1917? In what ways did relations with other countries change?

Turning Point

Forced by the growing pressure to turn the economic momentum around and by overall unpopularity, Tsar Nicholas II stepped out of office. He gave his leadership role to his younger brother; however, he would not accept it without the vote of the people. Out of necessity the Russian Provisional Government was assembled in Petrograd to form some type of leadership.

Turing Point Explanation

The time of the resignation of Tsar Nicholas II is the first radical change of the Russian Revolution, but it also marks the end of tsarist rule in Russia. This created a need for a political change to sustain the government, leading into the Russian Provisional Government. Although this occurred during the February Revolution, these events allowed the happenings of the October Revolution to take place, thus completing the entire Revolution of 1917. This time period is a turning point because it started the transformation and provided an outlet for the following events to occur. Without these events it would have been extremely difficult for Lenin and his followers to procure leadership.

Author Profile Format

For each focus work it is important to complete an Author Profile. If you cannot find the recommended biography in your local library, feel free to substitute any short biography that you find. I suggest using biographies found in the middle-grade or young adult sections of the library, as they usually provide an adequate introduction to the author's life without dwelling unnecessarily on the less savory bits.

Name (including pseudonyms if any)

Birth Date   Place

Death Date   Place

Best-Known Works

Include three or more of the author's best or best-known works.

Brief Biography

- How does this author use his or her personal experiences in his or her work?
- What current events or public figures affected the author's life and writing?
- How do the places in the author's life show up in his or her writing?

Author Profile Model

Name: Washington Irving (pseudonyms include Dietrich Knickerbocker, Jonathan Oldstyle, and Geoffrey Crayon)

Birth Date: April 3, 1783 **Place:** Manhattan, NYC, NY

Death Date: November 28, 1859 **Place:** Sunnyside, Irvington, NY

Best-Known Works

- *The Legend of Sleepy Hollow, Rip Van Winkle, The Sketchbook of Geoffrey Crayon, The Life of George Washington, Knickerbocker's History of New York*

Brief Biography

Washington Irving used his experiences living in both Europe and America to write humorous and meditative stories popular in both the new and old worlds. Irving's life and work were influenced by the events of the Revolutionary War and the War of 1812, and he was also profoundly influenced by other writers (both European and American) of his time. His favorite childhood stories involved voyages to far-off lands. The places of Irving's life show up extensively in his writing. He wrote of England, America, and even lived in Tarrytown, New York, where he set *The Legend of Sleepy Hollow*.

Literature Summary Format

Novel or Story Title: Write the story's full title and subtitle, if any, here.

Author: Write the author's full name and pseudonym, if any.

Theme: What is the main idea that the author wants to convey? The theme is the big idea illustrated by the story's plot and characters. This can often be expressed in a proverb or phrase such as "honesty is the best policy" or "love never fails."

Characterization: WHO is the story about, and what are they like? How does the author show you this?

Plot: WHAT happens in the story?

Setting: WHEN and WHERE does the story take place?

Style: HOW does the author create a mood and tell the story?

Literature Summary Model

Novel or Story Title: "The Secret Life of Walter Mitty"

Author: James Thurber

Theme

"The Secret Life of Walter Mitty" explores the desire of every human being to be smarter, braver, and more important, and what happens when this fantasy world becomes an addiction more real than reality itself.

Characterization

Walter Mitty is humanity taken to an extreme. He is a daydreamer, imagining he is a Navy pilot flying through the most devastating hurricane in history when he is just driving his wife to her hair appointment, or envisioning himself as a world-renowned surgeon when he drives past a hospital. You also get the feeling that Walter may be aging and not "all there."

Plot

"The Secret Life of Walter Mitty" chronicles a day in Mitty's life and his struggles to complete his daily routine instead of slipping into his fantasy world.

Setting

The setting of 1940s England has very little effect on the story, except that certain buildings Mitty passes do occasionally prompt certain daydreams.

Style

The story is handled with a rather straightforward, simple style that changes for each daydream. For example, when he imagines himself as a combat pilot, the characters speak with an efficient, clipped style, using only as many words as are necessary.

Literary Analysis Model

The format instructions for this model are found in the chapters on "How to Read a Book" and "How to Write an Essay." You will find this model helpful for most of the essays assigned throughout the curriculum. Additional models for specific types of essays can be found in the Excellence in Literature *Handbook for Writers*.

Student Name

Date

Class Name

Module # and Focus Text Title

Prompt

Pride and Prejudice was originally titled *First Impressions*. Consider both titles in relation to the characters of Elizabeth, Darcy, and Mr. Wickham, as well as to Austen's depiction of social class. What are the roles of pride, prejudice, and first impressions in the development of relationships among these characters and their social circles? What does Austen seem to suggest about pride, prejudice, and first impressions? Be sure to note Austen's use of irony, and provide specific textual support for your thesis.

The Defects of Human Nature

Life in the early 1800s revolved primarily around the social aspects of life. Social conventions ruled the actions of young ladies and their mothers, guided their brothers in selecting a spouse, and even dictated with whom their families were permitted to associate. Jane Austen gently ridicules the rigid structure of her society's rules and regimens in her novel *Pride and Prejudice*. Through her ironic situations and comical views of life, she attempts to reveal some of society's faults and offer alternatives for the faulty tendencies of human nature.

Pride was an integral part of the nineteenth-century culture. At the very foundation of the separations between social classes, pride enabled entire families to choose not to associate with each other so as not to damage their own social reputations. Mr. Darcy, "a fine figure of a man" with "ten thousand [pounds] a year" (16), embodied this pride admirably. During the first ball he attended in Hertfordshire, his air of superiority proved that he was assuredly aware that his fortune was much larger than anyone's in the room and that his social status was accordingly higher. His reclusive nature and manners also added to the aura of pride which enveloped him.

Although his neighbors were gentlemen and gentlemen's daughters, Mr. Darcy believed that his income and social standing in London set him above the residents of Hertfordshire. Indeed, later he acknowledged that his parents "almost taught [him] to be selfish and overbearing—to care for none beyond [his] own family circle, to think meanly of all the rest of the world, to wish at least to think meanly of their sense and worth compared with [his] own" (274).

Mr. Darcy further displayed the pride which was so deeply ingrained in him when he bungled his first proposal to Elizabeth Bennet. Although he began acceptably with expressions of his love, "he was not more eloquent on the subject of tenderness than of pride" (149). The descriptions of his admiration soon turned to illustrations of the obstacles he overcame to stand before her and propose. Despite his intended purpose to depict the depth of his emotion, his expressions of "his sense of her inferiority ... of the family obstacles which judgment had always opposed to inclination" (149) only served to anger and insult Elizabeth. Mr. Darcy's pride prevented him from understanding that the differences in social standing were evident to Elizabeth and that she would not be flattered by his explanations.

Although Elizabeth was not proud in the same manner as Mr. Darcy, she was not immune to human faults. Elizabeth's flaw was expressed in the more socially acceptable form of prejudice. Elizabeth discovered the danger of relying on first impressions as her relationships with Mr. Darcy developed. Mr. Darcy's actions at their first meeting prompted her to accept her community's harsh opinion of him as her own. Without making the effort to get to know Mr. Darcy, Elizabeth fixed her own views about his character and held "no very cordial feelings towards him" (17).

Elizabeth then repeated her mistake of allowing her impressions to turn into prejudice when she met Mr. Wickham. "... Struck with [Mr. Wickham's] air" (63) she formed her acquaintance with an inclination to approve of his actions. This inclination caused her to believe Mr. Wickham explicitly when he fabricated tales about Mr. Darcy. It reached to the extent that her friend felt the need to advise her not to "allow her fancy for Wickham to make her appear unpleasant in the eyes of a man of ten times his consequence" (77).

Ironically, Elizabeth did not begin to alter her prejudices until she accused Mr. Darcy of causing Mr. Wickham's "misfortune" (150). Mr. Darcy's account of the matters forced her to reverse her opinions about him and Mr. Wickham. "Every lingering struggle in [Mr. Wickham's] favor grew fainter and fainter" (161) as she recognized his indecent behavior and consequently scolded herself for not identifying them sooner. This discovery of the true character of these gentlemen was humiliating to Elizabeth as she had "prided [herself] on [her] discernment" (162). However painful this lesson may have been, Elizabeth benefited from it by gaining insight into the hazards of prejudice.

Although Jane Austen first titled her novel *First Impressions*, her final choice of *Pride and Prejudice* seems to fit her analysis of human behavior more suitably. Her humorous novel prodded her contemporaries to formulate their own opinions and not to rely on society's poor abilities or their own preconceived notions about themselves. It forced their descendants to confront their own human nature and face their personal defects.

Sample Compare/Contrast Essay Model

(NOTE: *This model contains spoilers for stories in Module 4.1, so you may want to read the stories before studying this example.*)

Student Name

Date

Class Name

Module # and Focus Text Title

Prompt: Choose two of the assigned stories, and write an essay comparing and contrasting ways in which the selected works are similar/different in one or two of the following areas: plot, theme, characterization, setting, and style.

Distinct Works of Art

"The Necklace" and "The Ransom of Red Chief" are two very different stories, and yet, when they are examined closely, a resemblance can be seen between them. The authors chose different ways to approach the stories, and very different character roles, but both produced well-written stories that captivate the reader's mind.

In "The Necklace," the plot is simple but interesting. The main character, Mathilde Loisel, receives an invitation to a party at the palace of Ministry, but is distressed by her lack of clothes and jewels to wear for the event. She buys a dress, and borrows a diamond necklace from Mme Forester. After the party, the necklace is nowhere to be found, but she can not bring herself to confess what had happened to Mme. Forester. Instead, she buys a necklace exactly like the one lent to her, which takes her ten years to pay for. During a friendly conversation with Mme. Forester years later, she discovers that the diamonds in the borrowed necklace were false.

The "Ransom of Red Chief" is created in a similar manner, with the story ending differently than the characters anticipated. In this rather amusing story, Bill and Sam kidnap a little boy Johnny, planning to ask money for the boy's return. The kidnappers thought that Johnny would be traumatized, and that Johnny's father, Ebenezer Dorest would be outraged by the boy's disappearance, but they were not. While being held hostage, Johnny entertains himself in the woods, playing Indians and Black Scouts with Bill and Sam. During the child's play, the men have some rather horrifying experiences while posing as Johnny's "Indian captives." They write to Mr. Dorset, demanding $1,500 for the boy's return as planned. In his reply, Mr. Dorset tells them that he will not pay the ransom, but will take Johnny off their hands for $250. Bill and Sam, aggravated by the little boy, pay the $250.

The plot itself is extremely different from The Necklace, but the story has similar results. In both cases, the characters did something that they knew was wrong, and in the end, rather than gaining something, they paid the consequences for their dishonesty or crime. Mathide Loisel would still have had to replace Mme. Forester's necklace, but would only have had the expense of false diamonds. In the Bill and Sam's case, if they had been truthful about their wrongdoing, it would have saved them the cost of bringing Johnny home.

Style is another focus in the stories. In The Necklace, the author uses dignified sounding words, which make graceful paragraphs throughout the story. It is written with such skill and craftsmanship that the reader is held in suspense until the end of the last paragraph. The very opposite of this writing style is found in The Ransom of Red Chief. Instead of using what might be thought of as "normal" speech, the characters use slang, and use imperfect grammar. Unlike The Necklace, it is an energetic and comical story that makes any reader twitch with even a slight smile.

These stories are both fabulous works of art, in which the characters learned valuable lessons. Although we may never be in a situation like the characters in the story, we can learn from them and apply the principles to our own lives.

Sample Poetry Analysis Model

Student Name

Date

Class Name

Module # and Focus Text Title

Prompt: Make a close reading of "God's Grandeur" or "The Windhover" by Gerard Manley Hopkins. Make sure you show how the images and figurative language in the poem complement one another. Show also how he uses sound, including consonance, assonance, and rhyme in constructing his poetic argument. Consider also how he develops his poetic argument from the beginning to the end of his poem.

Inspired by a Falcon

In "The Windhover," Gerard Manley Hopkins talks about watching a kestrel, a small falcon which hovers in the air. Dedicated to Christ, this poem celebrates the majesty, beauty, and power of one of God's creations. Hopkins describes the kestrel's flight, hovering, and dive, as well as his reaction to this display of strength. He is clearly awed, for "[his] heart …Stirred for a bird" (7–8).

Hopkins uses figurative language and imagery throughout "The Windhover." The title itself conveys the image of the kestrel hovering in the wind. In addition, the sounds of the poem correspond with its action.

In the first stanza Hopkins describes the kestrel's steady flying and gliding, as well as the poet's own admiration. The poem begins with "I caught this morning morning's minion, king- / dom of daylight's dauphin, dapple-dawn-drawn Falcon," (1–2).

The word "caught" is used figuratively, as in seen. The word "minion" means darling, and "Dauphin" is the title for the prince who is the heir to the French throne; Hopkins is acknowledging that the kestrel is the darling and ruler of the daylight. He admires "the achieve of, the mastery of the thing!" (7–8), as the kestrel flies uninhibited, master of flying and the air. Hopkins's use of the words "riding" (2) and "striding" (3) help us to see the image of the kestrel flying through the air. In addition, these words give us a sense of the kestrel moving smoothly with a sense of rhythm, which meshes well with his later image of skating. The kestrel glides or hovers through the air, just "As a skate's heel sweeps smooth on a bow-bend" (6).

This stanza has a rhythm that swings along, heightened by alliteration, assonance, and consonance, as in "dapple-dawn-drawn[.]" Later in the stanza Hopkins uses alliteration again to produce a smooth sound that imitates gliding. In addition, the way every line rhymes (they all end with "-ing") also emphasizes rhythm.

In the next stanza Hopkins is talking about the kestrel flying up and then diving down. He uses figurative language to convey the action. "Brute beauty and valour and act, oh, air, pride, plume, here / Buckle! AND the fire that breaks from thee" (9–10). Hopkins describes the kestrel by its attributes, and the combined effect is an impression of soaring and climbing. The bird is not "valour and act … air, pride, plume," but it and its flight embody those ideas. "Buckle!" and its possible meanings are a one-word summary of what is happening: to get ready, to make fast, to fall through. The poem builds up speed and dives with the windhover. Hopkins uses lots of different consonants and vowels to create a jumbled sound of words climbing upon one another, building up to "Buckle!" just as the kestrel climbs up and then dives. The "fire that breaks from [the kestrel]" refers to the way the kestrel's wings flash open, revealing a reddish-brown color, as the bird nears the ground. Later in the stanza Hopkins refers to the windhover as a "chevalier" (11), which conveys the idea of nobility and strength and "valour" (9). A knight gallops across the countryside; the kestrel hovers and dives in the sky.

In the last stanza the poem flies swiftly and easily to the ground with the bird. This stanza is more quiet; Hopkins uses soft-sounding vowels and consonants. "Sheer plod make plough down sillion / Shine" (12–13) has smooth consonants that move steadily forward just like a plow. Hopkins compares this to the way the kestrel plows through the air. Matching with the earlier figurative language of fire, Hopkins presents an image of "blue-bleak embers, ah my dear, [that] / Fall, gall themselves, and gash gold-vermilion." The embers are falling, opening, and glowing. This helps us to see the image of the kestrel diving through the sky and flashing open his reddish-brown wings when he nears the ground, just as the embers "gash gold-vermilion." In the last line, "Fall, gall themselves, and gash gold-vermilion" (14), even though the g's are hard, the vowel sounds; particularly the use of ah (definitely an example of assonance), soften the line.

Throughout "The Windhover," Hopkins's awe is evident in his enthusiastic description. He conveys his message with words and sounds that echo and emphasize his story, making it a poem of both visual images and oral expression. He uses this method to involve and engage the reader in his experience. Hopkins's soaring poetry shares his awe of the kestrel and its Creator with the reader.

MLA Format Model

Use these format guidelines for all of your Week 3/4 assignments.

Your Name

Date

Class Name

Module # and Focus Text Title

For an EIL essay, please add the writing prompt at this point.

Making Your Essay Look Good:
The Basics of MLA Format

In the upper right-hand corner of each page, beginning with page two if you prefer, one-half inch from the top (the text of your essay should begin one inch from the top), place a header with your last name, a space, and the page number. In most word-processing programs, you can do this from the "View" menu by selecting "Header and Footer." [NOTE: This is not shown in these models, but should be done in your own essays.] You should have one-inch margins on the right, the left, and the bottom of your page, and your essay should be double-spaced (set line spacing in your word processing program—do *not* place a hard return at the end of each line). Use one space at the end of terminal punctuation.

When you quote poetry, if the quotation is three or fewer lines, fit it right into your text. For instance, if I want to let you know that Blake begins "The Ecchoing Green" by juxtaposing "merry bells [that] ring / To welcome the spring" and "The sky-lark and thrush, / The birds of the bush," I would do it like I just did it. I might also note that Blake emphasizes this juxtaposition by the rhyme of "ring" and "sing," a rhyme that helps connect the natural and the human worlds because the sound describing the voices of the birds in the green echoes the sound describing the voice of human-made bells.

Notice that I keep the punctuation and the upper-case letters as they are in the poem. If I want to add something to make the quotation fit the grammar of my sentence, I do so by indicating the addition with brackets. If I wanted to leave something out of the poem and pick up the quotation a few words later, I would use ellipses, which are three dots with spaces between them (. . .).

I might then want to point out that, while "Old John" chimes in to the "merry" sounds as he "laugh[s] away care," the second stanza of the poem suggests his aging, and thus his experience of life, which might subtly trouble the innocence of the green. To show my point, I might quote the first five lines of the second stanza, though I might then find myself drifting from the close attention required in a solid analysis. If I take that chance of inattention, I would indent each line ten spaces and reproduce the lines of the poem just as they appear in the text. I would do this because I am quoting four or more lines of poetry. So the quotation would look like this:

      Old John with white hair

      Does laugh away care,

      Sitting under the oak,

      Among the old folk.

      They laugh at our play, . . .

After this, I had better make some particular observations about the language of the excerpt that I just quoted.

Remember, your essay's title is not the same as the title of the work you discuss in the essay. Your title has no quotation marks unless you have a quotation in it; neither is it underlined. Use quotation marks for the title of a short poem, essay, or short story. Italicize (or underline) the title of a book, a play, or a long poem—Wordsworth's *Prelude*, for instance.

In quoting prose, if the quotation takes up more than three lines of your text, you should indent the entire block ten spaces. Do not use ellipses (three periods separated by spaces) at the beginning or the end of the quotation; use them in the middle of the quotation to indicate you have removed words that are not essential to your point. Be sure to introduce all quotations with appropriate tags, blending quotations into your own sentence structure, grammar, and syntax. Punctuate quotations and cite page numbers as I do in the following sentence: DuBois begins his essay by depicting and defining the internalized "contempt and pity" of African-American "double-consciousness" (38); he ends the essay by turning that contempt and pity back upon the white America, a "dusty desert of dollars and smartness" (43). Notice that the end punctuation follows the page citation and is not within the quotation itself. Notice also that only the page number is within the parentheses. I would include an author's name only if the particular author was not clear from context.

If you have further questions about MLA style, look in the library for a copy of the *MLA Handbook for Writers of Research Papers,* use a writing handbook such as the Excellence in Literature *Handbook for Writers,* or visit the website below.

https://owl.english.purdue.edu/owl/resource/747/01/

Note: *This sample essay was provided courtesy of Dr. Robert Grotjohn, Professor Emeritus of English, Mary Baldwin College. It was one of the most helpful documents I received while in college, and I used it as a model for nearly every essay I wrote. I hope you find it equally helpful.*

How to Evaluate Writing

"You can always edit a bad page. You can't edit a blank page."

—Jodi Picoult

Grading papers is usually not a favorite chore, but have you ever thought of writing evaluation as a teaching tool? That is exactly what it can be! Every writing assignment and every evaluation can help a student grow as a writer, as long as the standards are clear and the evaluation is constructive and designed to teach. In addition, good evaluations help your student learn how to self-evaluate, which is a skill they will need in college and beyond.

A Constructive Evaluation Starts With a Rubric

What is a rubric? It's a checklist of objective standards. For a student, a rubric defines exactly what the teacher or writing mentor will be checking. Each item on the checklist is a clue as to how to meet the standard. For example, the first Content standard on the EIL rubric is "The essay contains a strong, easily identified thesis." This is a reminder to make sure this is true before you turn in the essay.

For parents and teachers, the rubric outlines what to check in three primary areas: Content (Ideas/Concepts and Organization) first, then Style (Voice, Sentence Fluency, and Word Choice), and finally, Mechanics (Conventions and Presentation). In each of these areas there are three or four specific goals or standards. Your job is to see how well your student meets these standards in each area.

Evaluation Priorities

When medics respond to a disaster with a large number of casualties, they "triage" or assign a level of urgency to each problem in order to know what to treat first. In a similar way, it makes sense to evaluate standards in order of importance. One way to think about it is to consider whether the most important part of a paper is WHAT is said, or HOW it is said, or whether everything is spelled correctly.

Because *what* the paper says is of first importance (if the ideas are muddled and illogically organized, all the style and perfect spelling in the world doesn't really matter), begin with Content standards, which evaluate Ideas/Concepts and Organization.

Next, look at *how* the ideas are communicated, including the Style standards of Voice, Sentence Fluency, and Word Choice. Finally, once the content, organization, and general style standards have reached an acceptable level, it will be time to focus on the standards of Mechanics, including grammar, presentation, and so forth.

If a student has many significant areas of difficulty, evaluate only the skills that have been specifically taught, and focus on only a few of the main items in each essay.

Parent Tip: How to Use a Writer's Handbook in Evaluation

A good writer's handbook makes it easy to offer specific, constructive feedback. If you have used a handbook such as the Excellence in Literature *Handbook for Writers*, you know that information is categorized into numbered paragraphs. These numbers allow you to direct the student to exactly the instruction he or she needs to fix an error or improve a skill.

> **1.8 Subject/Verb Agreement**
>
> In any clause, the subject must agree with the verb; that is, a singular subject has a singular verb, and a plural subject has a plural verb. Make sure you do not become confused by some word between the subject and the verb. Notice the following examples.
>
> *The collection of fifty guns has been stolen.*
>
> [The subject is "collection."]
>
> *The disease which infected the trees is root rot.*
>
> [The subject is "disease."]

For example, if your student is having difficulty with subject/verb agreement, you would look in the table of contents of the *Handbook for Writers* and find that subject/verb agreement appears in section 4.8 on page 242.

On the student's paper, underline the incorrect subject/verb combination and note the handbook section number in the margin. When you return the paper, the student should visit the handbook, read the assigned instructional paragraph, look at the examples, and see how to correct the error. Giving feedback this way is quick and efficient, and best of all, so much more helpful than just telling the student to be sure that the subject and verb agree.

How to Evaluate the First Draft
First draft priorities: Ideas/Concepts and Organization

After you do an initial read-through of the student's rough draft, get your writer's handbook and a copy of the rubric and evaluate the two Content skills, Ideas/Concepts and Organization.

I realize it is counter-intuitive for many parents to evaluate only the Content standards, because you will see mechanical errors or style problems in the rough draft. However, until the content and organization of the piece are finalized, there is little point in tweaking word choice or sentence fluency. Working at first with just the content helps keep attention on the first draft priorities of ideas and organization, and avoids the distraction of too much red ink.

How to Evaluate a Final Draft
Final draft priorities: Content, Style, and Mechanics (all standards)

When you receive a revised draft, read through it quickly to gain an overall impression. Have the changes you discussed in the previous draft been satisfactorily made? Use a fresh copy of the rubric to assess each of the seven skill areas and provide a feedback number or symbol for each characteristic listed.

For each draft, return the student's paper with a filled-out rubric, a brief note highlighting the positive and negative things you noticed about the paper, and handbook section numbers so the student can look up challenging items.

Should You Require More than Two Drafts?
Two drafts—a first and a final—are all I recommend. Writing skills improve with each new assignment, and moving through the assignments in a timely manner ensures that students will not get bogged down and end up disliking one of the classics or skipping the last few assignments of the year.

This section adapted from *Evaluate Writing the Easy Way* by Janice Campbell.

Excellence in Literature Evaluation Rubric

Name: Assignment:	Date: Evaluator:
Content: Ideas and Concepts _ The essay contains a strong, easily identified thesis. _ Interesting ideas and a compelling perspective hold the reader's attention. _ Relevant anecdotes, appropriate quotes, and specific details support the writer's position and demonstrate understanding of the prompt.	**Content: Organization** _ The structure of the paper enhances the presentation of the thesis and supporting ideas. _ Clear transitions move the reader easily from idea to idea. _ Quotes and textual support are blended smoothly, with correct tenses and formatting.
Style: Voice _ The writer speaks directly to the reader, using an appropriate tone and level of formality. _ The writer's voice is individual and engaging, providing a sense of the writer's personality. _ The writer demonstrates awareness of and respect for the audience and purpose of the writing.	**Mechanics: Conventions** _ Standard writing conventions (spelling, punctuation, capitalization, grammar, usage, paragraphing) are observed. _ Citations are correctly formatted using the MLA standard. _ Mechanical or typographical errors are few; only minor touch-ups needed.
Style: Sentence Fluency _ Sentences flow easily with graceful transitions. _ Sentences have a pleasant, appropriate rhythm and cadence when read aloud. _ Sentence structure is varied, with appropriate use of simple, complex, and compound sentences.	**Mechanics: Presentation** _ Essay is in MLA format: Times-New Roman font, 12 pt., 1" margins. _ Paper header with student, class, instructor, and date included. _ Essay prompt included after header and before title. _ Single space following all terminal punctuation.
Style: Word Choice _ Chosen words clearly convey the intended message. _ The words used are precise, interesting, powerful, engaging, and natural. _ The vocabulary is vivid and varied, though not necessarily exotic.	**Comments and Handbook Lookups**

Rating Scale
- ❏ 5 or + indicates that your essay demonstrated outstanding mastery in this area.
- ❏ 4 indicates that the essay is above average.
- ❏ 3 or = indicates that your essay was average and met assignment expectations in this area.
- ❏ 2 indicates that your essay was below average in this area.
- ❏ 1 or - indicates that you should write down this skill as a goal area for improvement.

Note: This rubric is intended for evaluation of the Week 3/4 assignments only. The shorter assignments from Weeks 1 and 2 are simply checked off on the pacing charts at the front of the book when each assignment is satisfactorily completed.

Excellence in Literature: Student Evaluation Summary

Student: **School Year:**

Grade: **English V: World Literature**

	Ideas/ Concepts	Organiza- tion	Voice	Word Choice	Sentence Fluency	Mechanics	Presen- tation	Total
Module 4.1- Homer								
Module 4.2- Sophocles								
Module 4.3- Virgil								
Module 4.4- Dante								
Module 4.5- Cervantes								
Module 4.6- Hugo								
Module 4.7- Russian authors								
Module 4.8- Goethe								
Module 4.9- Dinesen								
Total								
Average								

Class Description

World Literature is a college-preparatory literature and composition course. Focus works, including novels, short stories, poetry, and drama have been selected for literary quality and for their place in the historic development of literature.

Context readings provide background information about the author, and historic, literary, and artistic context of the focus work. Students will practice the skills of close literary analysis through essays, approach papers, and other types of writing.

Course Objectives

By the end of the course, students will:

- Understand the process of writing, including the use of tools such as a writer's handbook, dictionary, and thesaurus.
- Have specific understanding of selected representative texts by major authors of the periods studied.
- Have a general understanding of the historical and cultural contexts of the works.
- Be able to analyze literary texts and present thoughtfully developed ideas in writing.
- Demonstrate competence in essay organization, style, and mechanics.
- Demonstrate competence in the MLA style of source documentation.

Evaluations

Student writing is evaluated using the Excellence in Writing evaluation rubric. Each paper is analyzed and evaluated in the following seven areas: Ideas and Concepts, Organization, Voice, Word Choice, Sentence Fluency, Mechanics, and Presentation. Course grade is based upon essays (65%), shorter assignments (20%), English and Vocabulary Notebook (10%), and studentship (5%).

Comments

Glossary

*"The difference between the almost right word and the right word is really a large matter—
it's the difference between the lightning bug and the lightning."*

Mark Twain

Allegory: A story in which ideas are represented or personified as actions, people, or things. Example: *Pilgrim's Progress* by John Bunyan.

Alliteration: The repetition of beginning consonant sounds through a sequence of words. Gerard Manley Hopkins is noted for using alliteration in lines such as "Fresh-firecoal chestnut-falls; finches' wings;" from "Pied Beauty."

Allude/Allusion: To make a reference, either implied or stated, to the Bible, mythology, literature, art, music, or history that relies on the reader's familiarity with the alluded-to work to make or reinforce a point in the current work.

Analogy: A comparison based upon similarities and relationships of things that are somewhat alike but mostly different. An analogy often makes a point-by-point comparison from a familiar object to an unfamiliar.

Antagonist: The character who opposes the main character (the protagonist).

Antithesis: A counter-proposition that denotes a direct contrast to the original proposition, balancing an argument for parallel structure.

Archetype: A plot pattern, such as the quest or the redeemer/scapegoat, or character element, such as the cruel stepmother, that recurs across cultures.

Argument: The reasons (claim, supporting points, and evidence) a writer provides in order to persuade a reader that an idea or thesis is correct.

Assonance: The repetition of vowel sounds in a series of words. Example: "The rain in Spain falls mainly on the plain" from *Pygmalion* by George Bernard Shaw.

Ballad: A narrative poem or song with a repeating refrain. A ballad often tells the story of a historical event or retells a folk legend. Example: "The Raven" by Edgar Allen Poe.

Beast Fable: Also known as a "beast epic," this is an often satirical, allegorical style in which the main characters are animals. It is often written as a mock epic. Example: *Animal Farm* by George Orwell.

Blank Verse: Poetry with regular, metrical, unrhymed lines, usually iambic pentameter.

Burlesque: Refers to ridiculous exaggeration in language, usually one that makes the discrepancy between the words and the situation or the character silly. For example, to have a king speak like an idiot or a workman speak like a king (especially, say, in blank verse) is burlesque. Similarly, a very serious situation can be burlesqued by having the characters in it speak or behave in ridiculously inappropriate ways. In other words, burlesque creates a large gap between the situation or the characters and the style with which they speak or act out the event.

Caricature: The technique of exaggerating for comic and satiric effect one particular feature of a subject, in order to achieve a grotesque or ridiculous effect. Caricatures can be created either through words or pictures.

Characterization: The artistic presentation of a fictional character.

Citation: A standardized reference to a source of information in a written work. The citation usually includes author, title, publisher, and so forth, in a specific format. In the MLA style of citation that we use with this curriculum, the citations appear as signal phrases in the body of the text, and a "works cited" list follows the text.

Climax: The turning point in fiction; the transition from rising to falling action.

Comedy: In literary terms a comedy is a story, often centered on love, that has a positive ending. It may or may not be humorous.

Conflict: A struggle between two opposing forces. The conflict usually forms the central drama in a fictional narrative, and can be man vs. man, man vs. God, man vs. nature, man vs. society, or even man vs. himself.

Consonance: An "almost rhyme" in which consonants agree, but the vowels that precede them differ. Example: word/lord, slip/slop.

Context: In EIL, the conditions and/or circumstances within which a work of literature has been created, including historical events, literary periods, artistic movements, etc.

Couplet: In poetry, a pair of rhyming lines often appearing at the end of a sonnet.

Denouement: Resolution or conclusion.

Diction: An author's word choices.

Didactic: Literature with a moralistic or instructive purpose.

Dystopian: A literary genre featuring a society, often but not always in the future, that is caused and/or characterized by profoundly negative things such as dehumanization, environmental disaster, societal decline, or tyranny. Dystopia is an antonym for utopia.

Elegy: A poem, usually written as a formal lament on the death of a person. In classical time an elegy was any poem written in elegiac meter. Example: "In Memory of W. B. Yeats" by W. H. Auden.

End Rhyme: The repetition of identical or similar sounds in two or more different words found at the end of poetic lines.

Epic: A long narrative poem that tells a story, usually about the deeds of a hero. Example: Beowulf.

Epigram: A brief saying or poem, often ironic or satirical.

Epigraph: A phrase, quotation, or poem that suggests something about the theme and is set at the beginning of a chapter or book.

Episodic fiction: A story composed at loosely connected episodes, usually centering on a central character or group of characters.

Epistolary Style: A novel composed of a series of letters.

Essay: A paper that takes a position on a topic.

Euphemism: The substitution of a socially acceptable word or expression in place of harsh or unacceptable language. Example: "Passed away" for "died."

Exposition: The part of the narrative structure in which the scene is set, characters introduced, and the situation established. It usually falls at the beginning of the book, but additional exposition is often scattered throughout the work.

Fable: A short story, usually featuring animals or other non-human characters, that illustrates a moral lesson. Example: Aesop's "The Crow and the Pitcher."

Falling Action: The portion of plot structure, usually following the climax, in which the problems encountered during the rising action are solved.

Figure of Speech: An intentional deviation from ordinary language use in order to produce an artistic or rhetorical effect. See Scheme and Trope.

Flashback: A plot device in which a scene from the fictional past is brought into the fictional present, often to explain or illustrate a character's next action.

Foot: A group of syllables that form a basic unit of poetic rhythm.

Foreshadow: Hints or clues about future events in a narrative.

Framed Narrative: A story or stories told within a narrative frame. Example: *The Canterbury Tales* by Geoffrey Chaucer. Chaucer has framed a vivid grouping of stories within the frame of a narrative about a group of pilgrims who are traveling to Canterbury.

Free Verse: Poetry that does not rhyme, has no set line length, and is not set to traditional meter.

Full Stop: A period or other punctuation mark that indicates the end of a sentence.

Genre: A category of classification for literature such as fiction, non-fiction, and so forth. Pronounced zhahn-ruh.

Gothic Novel: A genre that evokes an aura of mystery and may include ghosts, dark and stormy nights, isolated castles, and supernatural happenings. Example: *Wuthering Heights* by Emily Brontë or *Frankenstein* by Mary Shelley.

Handbook: A writer's handbook such as the *Handbook for Writers* from Excellence in Literature, *Write for College*, *Writer's Inc.* from Write Source, or *Writer's Reference* by Diana Hacker.

Heroic Couplet: Two rhymed lines in iambic pentameter, forming a complete thought. This form was often used by Alexander Pope.

Homonym/Homophone: Words that sound much the same but have different meanings, origins, or spelling.

Hubris: A term derived from the Greek language that means excessive pride. In Greek tragedy and mythology, hubris often leads to the hero's downfall.

Hyperbole: Overstatement through exaggerated language.

Imagery: Words, phrases, and sensory details used to create a mood or mental picture in a reader's mind. Example: From "Mariana" by Alfred, Lord Tennyson:
"With blackest moss the flower-plots
Were thickly crusted, one and all;
The rusted nails fell from the knots
That held the pear to the gable wall.
The broken sheds looked sad and strange:
Unlifted was the clinking latch;
Weeded and worth the ancient thatch
Upon the lonely moated grange . . . "

Iambic Pentameter: In poetry, a metrical pattern in a ten-syllable line of verse in which five unaccented syllables alternate with five accented syllables, with the accent usually falling on the second of each pair of syllables.

Irony: A stylistic device or figure of speech in which the real meaning of the words is different from (and opposite to) the literal meaning. Irony, unlike sarcasm, tends to be ambiguous, bringing two contrasting meanings into play.

Literary Device:

Manners: A novel of manners focuses on and describes in detail the social customs and habits of a particular social group. Examples include *Pride and Prejudice* by Jane Austen and *Age of Innocence* by Edith Wharton.

Metaphor: A comparison between two objects, not using the terms "like" or "as."

Meter: The pattern of stressed and unstressed syllables in a line of poetry.

Mock Heroic: A satiric style which sets up a deliberately disproportionate and witty distance between the elevated language used to describe an action or event and the triviality or foolishness of the action (using, for example, the language of epics to describe a tea party). The mock heroic style tends to be an inside joke, in that it appeals to the sophistication of a reader familiar with the epic original but is not understood by readers who are not familiar with the traditional epic form. It encourages the reader to see the ridiculousness of the heroic pretensions of trivial people and is thus an excellent vehicle for skewering the sin of pride. Example: "Mac Flecknoe" by John Dryden or Pope's "Rape of the Lock."

Motif: A recurrent device, formula, or situation, often connecting a fresh idea with common patterns of existing thought.

Myth: A type of story that is usually symbolic and extensive, including stories shared across a culture to explain its history and traditions. Example: "Romulus and Remus."

Narrator: The character who tells the story. This may or may not be the hero, and the narrator may be reliable (trustworthy) or unreliable. Example: Ishmael in *Moby Dick*.

Nature: As it refers to a person, this is used to identify something inborn or inherent, e. g. "human nature" that often leads to predictable actions.

Octave: In poetry, the first eight lines of the Italian, or Petrarchan, sonnet.

Ode: A lyric poem with a serious topic and formal tone but without formal pattern. This form was especially popular among the Romantic poets. Example: "Ode to the West Wind" by Percy Bysshe Shelley.

Omniscient Point of View: In literature, a narrative perspective from multiple points of view that gives the reader access to the thoughts of all the characters.

Onomatopoeia: The formation or use of a word that sounds like what it means. Example: hiss; sizzle; pop.

Oxymoron: A figure of speech that combines two seemingly contradictory elements. Example: living death; sweet sorrow.

Parable: A short story with an explicit moral lesson. Example: The parable of the sower (Matthew 13:18–30).

Paradox: A statement that may appear contradictory but is actually true. Example: "Less is more."

Parody: A style of writing that deliberately seeks to ridicule another style, primarily through exaggeration.

Pastoral: Poem or play that describes an idealized, simple life that country folk, usually shepherds, are imagined to live in a world full of beauty, music, and love.

Personification: To endow a non-human object with human qualities. Example: Death in "Death Be Not Proud" by John Donne.

Picaresque: A style of novel that features a loosely connected series of events, rather than a tightly constructed plot, often with a non-traditional hero. Example: *Moll Flanders* by Daniel Defoe.

Plagiarism: To plagiarize is to copy or borrow the work or ideas of another author without acknowledgment. It is both unethical and illegal. When you are writing anything, such as essays, reports, dissertations, or creative works, you must cite your sources of information, including books, periodicals, or online resources, within your text as well as in a list of references appended to the work.

Plot: The sequence of narrated events that form a story.

Poetic Justice: A literary device in which virtue is ultimately rewarded or vice punished.

Point of View: The perspective from which people, events, and other details in a story are viewed.

Protagonist: The main character in a work, either male or female.

Pseudonym: A false name used to disguise a writer's identity. Example: Mary Anne Evans used the pseudonym George Eliot.

Pun: A wordplay that exploits the double meaning or ambiguity in a word to create an amusing effect. Example: The title of *The Importance of Being Earnest* by Oscar Wilde.

Quest: A type of literary plot that focuses on a protagonist's journey toward a difficult goal. There may or may not be a physical journey involved. Example: Homer's *Odyssey*; J. R. R. Tolkien's *The Lord of the Rings*.

Realism: A type of literature that tries to present life as it really is.

Reductio ad absurdum: A popular satiric technique in which the author agrees enthusiastically with the basic attitudes or assumptions he wishes to satirize and, by pushing them to a logically ridiculous extreme, exposes the foolishness of the original attitudes and assumptions. Example: "A Modest Proposal" by Jonathan Swift.

Refrain: A phrase, line, or group of lines that is repeated throughout a poem, usually after every stanza.

Regional literature: Fiction or poetry that emphasizes setting through colorful details, including dialect, dress, customs, landscape features, and history, of a specific, often rural, place and the people who inhabit it.

Reliable narrator: See "Narrator."

Resolution: The point of closure to the conflict in the plot.

Rhetoric: The art of using language to persuade or influence others. Sometimes includes the idea of eloquence (an older meaning) or of insincerity or artificiality in language (more modern interpretation). Examples: Mark Antony's speech in *Julius Caesar* by William Shakespeare or the character of Squealer in *Animal Farm* by George Orwell.

Rhyme Scheme: The pattern of end rhymes in a poem, noted by small letters, e.g., abab or abcba, etc.

Rising Action: The part of the plot structure in which events complicate or intensify the conflict, or introduce additional conflict.

Romance: A type of novel that presents an idealized picture of life. A novel of romance can be considered almost the opposite of a novel of realism. If you were expecting that the definition of "romance" would have something to do with love, you may want to look at the definition of "comedy" instead.

Rubric: A checklist for scoring that includes guidelines for expectations.

Sarcasm: A form of verbal irony in which apparent praise is actually criticism. Example: "A modest little person, with much to be modest about." Winston Churchill

Satire: A composition in verse or prose that uses humor, irony, sarcasm, or ridicule to point out vice or folly in order to expose, discourage, and change morally offensive attitudes or behaviors. It has been aptly described as an attack with a smile. Example: "A Modest Proposal" by Jonathan Swift.

Scansion: The process of analytically scanning a poem line by line to determine its meter.

Scheme: A rhetorical device or figure of speech in which words or phrases are put together in a manner that is different in syntax, sequence, or pattern from ordinary usage. Example: alliteration, in which a series of words features repetition of consonant sounds, e. g. "And churlish chiding of the winter's wind/ Which, when it bites and blows upon my body" from *As You Like It* by William Shakespeare.

Setting: The time and place in which the action of a story, poem, or play takes place.

Simile: A comparison of two things, using the words "like" or "as." Example: "My love is like a red, red rose . . . " by Robert Burns.

Soliloquy: A monologue in which a character talks to himself. Example: Hamlet's "To be or not to be . . . " soliloquy.

Sonnet: A fixed verse form consisting of fourteen lines, usually in iambic pentameter. Variations include Italian (Petrarchan), Shakespearean, and Spenserian.

Stanza: A section of a poem, preceded and followed by an extra line space.

Stereotype: A characterization based on the assumption that a personal trait such as gender, age, ethnic or national identity, religion, occupation, or marital status is predictably accompanied by certain characteristics, actions, even values.

Stock Character: A flat character sketch that fills a classic, easily understood role without much detail. Example: The wicked stepmother in *Cinderella*.

Stream of Consciousness: A modern writing style that replicates and records the random flow of thoughts, emotions, memories, and associations as they rush through a character's mind. Example: *To the Lighthouse* by Virginia Woolf.

Structure: The arrangement of the various elements in a work.

Style: A distinctive manner of expression distinguished by the writer's diction, rhythm, imagery, and so on.

Summary titles: A style of title in which the author offers a mini preview of the events of the chapter. Usually one sentence in length; often begins with "In which . . .".

Syllabus: An outline of course requirements. In *Excellence in Literature*, the syllabus is this book in its entirety.

Symbol: A person, place, thing, event, or pattern in a literary work that is not only itself but also stands for something else, often something more abstract. Common symbolism includes darkness as a representation of confusion or evil; a storm as foreboding or a threat; or beauty as a symbol of virtue. This PDF may help you understand symbols: http://goo.gl/gGLU4O

Syntax: The rules of grammar and style that govern the arrangement of words and phrases in order to create well-structured sentences.

Textual Support: Brief quotes from a text that is being analyzed. These quotes should usually be smoothly integrated into an original, analytical sentence.

Theme: The main idea or dominant concern of a novel, play, or poem stated in a generalized, abstract way. Example: "Crime does not pay." "Honesty is the best policy."

Thesis: A sentence or statement that summarizes the main idea of any argument and the premise or position that you are arguing.

Tone: The attitude a novel or poem takes toward its subject.

Tragedy: A story in which the character begins at a high point but ends badly, often because of a fatal flaw in his character that causes him to make poor choices. Example: *King Lear* by William Shakespeare; *Oedipus Rex* by Sophocles.

Tragic Flaw: An error in judgment, accidental wrongdoing, or unwitting mistake that results in tragedy, derived from the Greek idea of *hamartia*, or missing the mark.

Tragic Hero: A character, often a noble person of high rank, who comes to a disastrous end in his or her confrontation with a superior force (fortune, the gods, social forces, universal values), but also comes to understand the meaning of his or her deeds and to accept an appropriate punishment.

Trope: A rhetorical device or figure of speech using a word or phrase that intentionally deviates from ordinary language. A metaphor is an example of a trope, as it describes an object or event as something that it clearly is not, in order to make a comparison. Example: "All the world's a stage."

Unreliable Narrator: A speaker or voice whose narration is consciously or unconsciously deceiving. This type of narration is often subtly undermined by details in the story or through inconsistencies with general knowledge.

Voice: The style, personality, and tone of a narrative; also the speaker or narrator. An appropriate voice captures the correct level of formality, social distance, and personality for the purpose of the writing and the audience.

Use the space below to record additional words and definitions you want to remember.

Selected Resources

There is an endless supply of books on reading, writing, and literature, but it can be difficult to find the best. As I look at my bookshelves, I see that many books boast an array of sticky-note flags. When I open them, I find extensive marginal notations, underlined passages, and occasionally, extra slips of paper left at especially important spots. Here are just a few of the well-thumbed volumes on my bookshelves, as well as a few e-resources you will find helpful.

NOTE: Although a few of these optional resources include a faith-based perspective, it is important to note that the Excellence in Literature curriculum approaches literature from a nonsectarian literary perspective. It is designed for use in any teaching setting.

A CiRCE Guide to Reading: This compact guide teaches a multi-layered, flexible approach to reading that includes elements of speed-reading, close reading, and humane reading.

Adventures in Art by David and Shirley Quine: This interactive e-text is designed to help you "visualize the significant changes in ideas throughout history, and then relate those changes to their cultural meaning."

American Passages: A Literary Survey: This well-organized site, designed to enhance the study of American literature, offers timelines, art, and other context information in an easily navigated format. One unique feature allows students to construct a multimedia slideshow of selected materials from the site; then use the slideshow for a presentation.

https://www.learner.org/series/american-passages-a-literary-survey/

"**Analyzing Poetry**" from Study Guide: http://www.studyguide.org/poetry_tips.htm

An Experiment in Criticism by C. S. Lewis: This is my top recommendation for a book on how to approach literature. In less than 150 pages, Lewis explains how to read various types of literature, and incidentally manages to offer hints on approaching music and art as well. Even though this is short, it is rich and well worth reading and re-reading.

Benét's Reader's Encyclopedia: This wonderful resource is described as "the classic and only encyclopedia of world literature in a single volume including poets, playwrights, novelists, and belletrists, synopses, historical data, major characters, in literature, myths and legends, literary terms, artistic movements, and prize winners." Any of the older editions will include the important elements of the Western literary tradition. I use it often.

The Company of the Creative: A Christian Reader's Guide to Great Literature and Its Themes by David L. Larson: This helpful, nonsectarian guide offers brief overviews of great authors and their work, plus useful recommendations for further reading.

Developing Linguistic Patterns Through Poetry Memorization by Andrew Pudewa: To write well, a student needs to internalize the rhythm and cadence of well-composed language. This book will help you accomplish that.

A Dictionary of Literary Symbols by Michael Ferber: This helpful guide, now available free online, "explains . . . literary symbols that we all frequently encounter (such as swan, rose, moon, gold), and gives hundreds of cross-references and quotations" from classic authors, the Bible, and English, American, and European literature.

https://www.academia.edu/37950209/Michael_Ferber_A_Dictionary_of_Literary_Symbols_Cambridge_University_Press_1999_pdf

Discovering Music: Dr. Carol Reynolds has created a "unique curriculum [that] takes you through the history of music, the arts, and Western Culture from 1600 to

1914" in about 13 hours of video instruction. This is an excellent context supplement to EIL. http://discoveringmusic.net/

The Elegant Essay Writing Lessons: Building Blocks for Analytical Writing by Lesha Myers: If a student needs extra help in essay writing, this simple guide can help. This may be used before or concurrently with Excellence in Literature.

Excellence-in-Literature.com: Here you will find many of the context resources and study references used in the *Excellence in Literature* curriculum and *Model-Based Writing*.

Excellence in Literature *Handbook for Writers*: The first half of this 400+ page handbook for student and teacher contains detailed instruction on essay writing, including a selection of sample outlines for different types of papers. The second half is a guide to usage and style, including sentence construction, word usage, punctuation, and more.

Gutenberg: Free Books: This wonderful site contains many classic books in digital form. I don't recommend reading on a screen unless you have to, but these book files might be useful if you cannot find a copy locally.

How to Read a Book: The Classic Guide to Intelligent Reading by Mortimer J. Adler and Charles Van Doren: There are multiple levels of reading—elementary, inspectional, and synoptical—and the authors clearly explain each and teach the reader how to appropriately read various types of literature.

How to Read and Why by Harold Bloom: A Yale professor and author of many books on literature, Bloom offers this brief volume of selections chosen not "as an exclusive list of what to read, but rather a sampling of works that best illustrate why to read." For a more extensive overview of the classics, you may want to read The Western Canon.

How to Read Slowly: Reading for Comprehension by James W. Sire: This is a concise introduction (just six chapters!) to reading literature from a worldview perspective.

Imitations in Writing: The Grammar of Poetry by Matt Whiting: This accessible text "focuses on teaching the fundamentals of poetry (figurative language, meter, rhyme, etc.) by means of imitation and review." We found it to be an easy-to-use introduction to poetry.

Invitation to the Classics: A Guide to Books You have Always Wanted to Read by Louise Cowan and Os Guinness: This attractive guide presents a chronological survey of great literature. The purpose of the book is to "introduce the Western literary masterworks in a clear and simple style that is mature in seriousness and tone and Christian in perspective—and in doing so, to help reawaken Western people to the vibrant heritage of these classics that are rich in themselves and in their two-thousand-year relationship to the Christian faith."

Librivox: Free Audio Books: The exciting thing about LibriVox is that you do not have to be content with just the books they offer—you can record and upload your own! The quality of these amateur recordings varies, but the price is right. http://librivox.org/

The Lifetime Reading Plan by Clifton Fadiman: Fadiman offers an overview of the Western canon, with brief discussions about each author and his or her greatest works. His aim is to help the reader "avoid mental bankruptcy" and to "understand something …of our position in space and time …[and] know how we got the ideas by which …we live."

Norton Anthologies: I recommend looking for used copies of the Norton Anthologies at used bookstores, remainder tables, or online, because they contain decent author introductions and their chronological format makes it easy to see the literary context of the works we will study throughout Excellence in Literature. Other anthologies may be useful, but I like the older Norton editions because they tend to stick with the classics. I suggest getting the American, English, World, and Poetry anthologies.

Writing About Literature: Norton's basic instruction in how to read analytically and write an analytical essay. This resource seems to move regularly. If this link does not work, try doing a web search for "Writing About Literature: Norton," and you may find it.

https://wwnorton.com/college/english/write/writesite/rhetoric/writing_about_lit.aspx

On Writing Well: An Informal Guide to Writing Nonfiction by William Zinsser- There is a good reason that this classic resource just celebrated its thirtieth anniversary with a new edition; it is an excellent model for its subject. Zinsser begins with an overview of writing principles, then moves into detailed discussion of forms and methods. It is a valuable resource for any writer.

The Politically Incorrect Guide to English and American Literature by Elizabeth Kantor, Ph.D. is an entertaining romp through selected English language literature. Overall, the book provides a memorable introduction to the ideas that have shaped the literary world, as well as sound recommendations for books you must not miss (most of them are included in the Excellence in Literature series).

Reading Between the Lines: A Christian Guide to Literature by Gene Edward Veith, Jr.: This interesting guide begins with a chapter on the importance of reading, then progresses through the forms, modes, and traditions of literature, with extensive end-notes for each chapter.

Vocabulary Study: If you enjoy vocabulary study and would like to add a vocabulary program to the contextual vocabulary study in EIL, Dynamic Literacy's *Word Build* program goes beyond the simple study of roots by using "morphology, the study of the units of meaning in words. [Just as] mastery of phonics helps students 'sound out' unfamiliar words; a mastery of morphics helps students 'mean out' unfamiliar words." An alternative is the *Vocabulary from Classical Roots* series, which presents Greek and Latin roots in a series of well-designed lessons.

Write for College: A Student Handbook: Specific instructions on many types of writing, plus a proofreader's guide to grammar, punctuation, and style, and much more. Younger students may prefer *Writer's INC*, which is similar, but for 11th–12th grades and beyond, *Write for College* or the EIL *Handbook for Writers* (referenced earlier) is most useful.

A Writer's Reference by Diana Hacker: I still turn to this brief handbook because of its handy tabbed format and helpful citation guides, including MLA and APA styles. It might be a useful supplement to either of the other suggested guides.

Word Processing Software

If you do not have a full-featured word processing program such as Microsoft Word, I recommend Google's free online suite of applications, including a word processor, spreadsheet program, and other tools. All you need for access to these is a free Google account, available at https://accounts.google.com/SignUp.

About the Author

*The greatest part of a writer's time is spent in reading,
in order to write; a man will turn over half a library to make one book."*
— Samuel Johnson

Janice Campbell, a lifelong reader and writer, loves to introduce students to great books and beautiful writing. She holds an English degree from Mary Baldwin College, and is the graduated homeschool mom of four sons.

Janice speaks at conferences nationwide on subjects including literature, writing, homeschool planning, high school records and transcripts, and other topics for homeschooling families, co-ops, and private schools. She is the author of the *Excellence in Literature* curriculum for grades 8-12, *Transcripts Made Easy*, and *Get a Jump Start on College*, and the publisher of a new edition of the 1857 McGuffey Readers with instructions for use with Charlotte Mason methods. In addition, she is an occasional host on the Homeschool Solutions podcast.

You'll find more of Janice's writing about reading, writing, and education from a Charlotte Mason/Classical perspective in various magazines and at her websites, EverydayEducation.com (the bookstore), Excellence-in-Literature.com (the literature resource site), and DoingWhatMatters.com (the blog). Whether you are homeschooling or teaching in a co-op or classroom, you're sure to find helpful tips and resources on all three sites.

www.ingramcontent.com/pod-product-compliance
Lightning Source LLC
Chambersburg PA
CBHW081826230426
43668CB00017B/2393